EMPATHY IN TRANS

A COMPARATIVE STUDY OF PO

IN TWO ENGLISH VERSIONS O

红楼梦诗词英译移情比较研究

李虹◎著

安徽师范大学出版社

· 芜湖 ·

图书在版编目(CIP)数据

《红楼梦》诗词英译移情比较研究 / 李虹著 . — 芜湖: 安徽师范大学出版社, 2020.9(2021.4重印)

ISBN 978-7-5676-3580-7

Ⅰ. ①红… Ⅱ. ①李… Ⅲ. ①《红楼梦》—古典诗歌—英语—翻译—对比研究 Ⅳ. ①H315.9

中国版本图书馆CIP数据核字(2018)第107107号

《红楼梦》诗词英译移情比较研究

HONGLOUMENG SHICI YINGYI YIQING BIJIAO YANJIU　　李虹　著

责任编辑: 吴　琼　　责任校对: 汪碧颖

装帧设计: 丁奕奕　　责任印制: 桑国磊

出版发行: 安徽师范大学出版社

芜湖市九华南路189号安徽师范大学花津校区

网　　址: http://www.ahnupress.com/

发 行 部: 0553-3883578　5910327　5910310(传真)

印　　刷: 苏州市古得堡数码印刷有限公司

版　　次: 2020年9月第1版

印　　次: 2021年4月第2次印刷

开　　本: 889 mm×1194 mm　1/32

印　　张: 8.25

字　　数: 240千字

书　　号: ISBN 978-7-5676-3580-7

定　　价: 39.00元

前　言

《红楼梦》是我国古典小说中一部最优秀的现实主义文学巨著，是曹雪芹经过"呕心沥血，披阅十载，增删五次"长期艰辛劳动才给子孙后世留传下来的一件宝贵的艺术珍品。自问世之后，它所具有的思想艺术魅力，立刻惊动了当时的社会。特别自19世纪中叶以来，《红楼梦》曾数次被译成外国文字，使其艺术成就享誉全球。

《红楼梦》的艺术价值是多方面的，不仅思想内容博大精深，而且语言"文备众体"，集多种文体于一体。其中诗歌体裁更是该小说中的精髓和一朵璀璨的奇葩，诗、词、曲、赋一应俱全，表现形式错落有致。诗歌的穿插巧夺天工，成为小说不可或缺的有机组成部分，与小说情节的发展和人物命运的演绎浑然一体。同时，诗歌又是作者寄予和阐发情感的绝佳形式。这为小说中故事情节的铺设增添了效果，彰显了作者高超的语言艺术；同时也给后来的翻译工作带来了非常大的难度，以至于有人认为如何翻译其中的诗歌部分往往成为判断《红楼梦》译本成败的关键。然而，翻译界对《红楼梦》各种译本中的诗歌翻译比较研究也很不全面，大多数学者集中在诗歌语言的可译性上。对于不同译者在翻译《红楼梦》中诗歌部分时是否也寄予了译者自身的情感，或者说，不同译者所呈现差异化的诗歌翻译形式是否因为译者移情差异所致，这一问题未曾有过系统深入的研究。因此，本书试图从移情视角来分析研究《红楼梦》不同译本中有关其诗歌翻译的特点和规律。

迄今为止已有二十余种《红楼梦》外文译本和节译本，其中影响最大的当属中国学者杨宪益和其夫人翻译的*A Dream of Red Mansions*以及英国汉学家霍克斯和其女婿翻译的*The Story of the Stone*（以下均简称为杨译和霍译）。这两个译本既是外国读者阅读、研究《红楼梦》的重要文本，也是我国翻译界进行翻译比较研究的重要素材。为此，本书的诗歌翻译均以杨译和霍译为素材。

《红楼梦》诗词翻译移情研究分三个方面：审美移情、文化移情和语用移情。通过对杨、霍两译本中的诗歌进行系统比较研究，发现二者在诗歌翻译中都存在移情现象，而且应用了不同的移情法，杨译主要移情于原文和原文作者，而霍译主要移情于译文与译文读者。本书试图从以下三个方面来解析这两种移情方式的差异：一是理论来源——目的论、阐释学和解构主义，这三个理论为此两种不同的移情法提供了理论上的支持。二是诗歌本身的特点，中文诗歌形式的生动性、简约性和含蓄性给拓展性阐释提供了客观语言基础，为多种翻译提供了可能条件。三是翻译的主观性，从二者的诗词翻译中可以看出，翻译并不具有许多翻译理论所宣称的那样“信”和“客观”，译者并不那样“中立”和“实事求是”，翻译过程中翻译主观性非但不可避免而且必不可少，因为翻译赖以存在的基础——语言，翻译赖以存在的主体——译者，都具有主观属性。当然，这种主观性不总是主观臆造，而是翻译中的一种思维过程和方式，是翻译主体主观能动性的一种表现。承认这种主观性不是对翻译客观性的否定，而是一种对翻译主观性的辩证态度。

Foreword

Hongloumeng is a masterpiece of classical novels in Chinese realism literature. It was written by Chaoxueqin, who had exerted painstaking efforts to revise it five times in ten years. After it became publicized, it immediately shook the society with its depth of thought and power of art. Since the mid-19th century, it has been translated into a number of foreign languages and thus has gained worldwide fame.

The artistic value of *Hongloumeng* is multiple: it lies not only in the richness of contents, but also in its successful integration with almost all the techniques of literary merits. Among them the poetic style is the soul and the splendid flower of the novel, for four genres (shi, ci, qu, fu) of Chinese poetic styles, closely related with the plot development and the characterization of the novel, are delicately scattered in the novel as an indispensable organic component of it. At the same time, the poems in the novel are superexcellent expressions of the writer's feelings as well. This approach both strengthens the effectiveness of plot development and brings out the writer's language art. However, it renders the translation of the poems difficult as well. So much so that some people even think how the poems of the novel are translated is a key factor in judging the success of the translation. Moreover, as far as I know, the comparative studies of *Hongloumeng*'s poetry translation are not comprehensive; most scholars focus their concern on the translatability. Research on how different translators release their own feelings on their translations of the poems has been inadequate; in other words, the issue whether the differences in different versions rendered by different translators are caused by their different empathy still awaits exploration. So, in this dissertation we will make a comparative study on the characteristics and rules of poetry translation in two different versions of *Hongloumeng* from the perspective of empathy.

Up to now, there have been more than 20 translations of the full text or abridged versions of *Hongloumeng*, two of which are best-known: the one translated by Yang Xianyi and his wife Gladys Yang (Yang's version for short), and the one by David Hawkes and his son-in-law John Minford (Hawkes' version for short). These two versions are both important texts for foreign readers and researchers, and key materials for comparative studies in the translation field. So, in this dissertation we will naturally base our study on these two versions.

The issue of empathy in translation will be approached from three perspectives: aesthetic empathy, cultural empathy and pragmatic empathy. After the comparative studies and analysis of the poems in *Hongloumeng*, we find that Yang and Hawkes both employ the approach of empathy in their translation of poetry. Yang mainly empathizes towards the author and the source text (ST for short); while Hawkes towards the readers and the target text (TT for short). Three possible explanations are proposed in the dissertation for such difference in translation. Firstly, theoretical explanations of empathy. Skopos theory, hermeneutics and deconstruction concept all justify theoretically the causes of the two different empathetic approaches of Yang's and Hawkes'. Secondly, features of Chinese poetic language. Vividness, succinctness and implicitness of Chinese poetic language allow for expansion and provide possibilities for the various versions of the same ST. Lastly, subjectivity of translation. From these two translators' practice, we can see that translation is not so "faithful" or "objective" as the translation theories advocate, translators can't stay "neutral", "practical or realistic" in the process of translation, subjectivity is not only inevitable but even indispensable, because the language (the foundation of translation) and the translator (the subject of translation) both bear subjectivity. Such subjectivity is not always a subjective conjecture but a thinking mode of translation, it is a manifestation of the subjective initiative of the translation subject. Admitting this subjectivity doesn't mean the denial of objectivity of translation but a dialectic attitude towards translation.

Contents

Introduction

Hongloumeng, one of China's greatest realistic novels, was written by Cao Xueqin (?—1763 or 1764) in the mid-eighteenth century during the reign of Emperor Qian Long of the Qing Dynasty (1644—1911). With its profound philosophy, panoramic picture of Chinese culture and refined language, it has received the highest accolade as one of the four classic masterpieces of Chinese literature and has contributed greatly to the world cultural treasure-house. As a classical Chinese novel it has been translated into many different languages and widely read and appreciated by the English speaking readers through the excellent translated versions, which embodies diversiform genres, among which the poetical style is also indispensable as an organic component of the whole novel. After its abridged and full renderings in other languages were published respectively since the 19th century, it has been "the most widely read Chinese novel in the Western world." (Poupard, 1984: 532) The boom helps to inspire the study on the greatest novel all around the world. However, it is really regrettable that the translation of its poetry is often neglected or paid less attention to. Such ignorance of poetry translation in *Hongloumeng* has not been meliorated until the 1970s when the two complete English versions, *The Story of the Stone* (hereinafter called Hawkes' version) translated by the British sinologist David Hawkes and his son-in-law John Minford and *A Dream of Red Mansions* (hereinafter called Yang's version) translated by the Chinese scholar Yang Xianyi and his wife Gladys Yang, were published. Up to now, these two translated versions have been the most popular ones in the world with very deep aesthetic and cultural values, and have been extensively studied both at home and abroad. The publication of the two versions contributes greatly to the intercultural communication between China and Western countries.

Nowadays, along with the appearance of these two translated versions, the research on poetry translation in *Hongloumeng* is rising. Differing from poetry in other novels, poetry in *Hongloumeng* has melted itself into the novel's background, plot, theme, etc. As an integral part of the whole novel, poetry is not only intertwined with the development of the theme, but also reflects the characters' personalities, indicates their destinies. Therefore, the study of poetry can facilitate the understanding of the novel. Also, poetry translation is generally held to be the most difficult and demanding form of translation, which deserves further study. In this thesis, the author chooses some of the poems and does a comparative study between Yang's and Hawkes' poetry translation from the perspective of empathy to illustrate possible explanations for their two different empathetic approaches by exemplifying how the translators empathize with the poets in their translation under the guidance of the approach of empathy.

The term empathy is of comparatively recent origin, and translates the late-nineteenth-century German coinage of *Einfühlung*, which has its origin in German aesthetics and originally means "reflecting or feeling into". Empathy is a complex concept that has been studied in different academic fields, such as aesthetics, psychology, linguistics, sociology and so on.

In the thesis, the author adopts the common empathetic approach as the guidance in the study of poetry translation in *Hongloumeng*. The concept of empathy is of great significance in poetry translation. As is well-known, empathy and translation are closely related. Empathy is considered as a kind of "transference" by the American Professor Susan Ingram that is closely related to "translate". Therefore, empathy is sometimes simply defined as "sentimental transference". Poetry comes from sentiments and depends on sentiments, so only by fully understanding the writer's sentiments can the translation work be done appealingly, and people are all blessed with common sentiments, which makes it possible for translators to express similar sentiments in another language. Therefore, the translation of poetry can be viewed as an empathetic process.

Apart from its introduction and conclusion, the whole thesis is made up of seven chapters. Chapter One is a general review over the development of empathy and previous studies in poetry translation in *Hongloumeng*. Chapter Two includes some theories related to poetry and poetry translation, such as the three elements of poetry, the translatability of poetry and basic issues for poetry translation. In Chapter Three, the application of the empathetic approach in poetry translation is the main topic. The difficulties of poetry translation due to linguistic, grammatical and cultural differences are mentioned and then the theoretical and practical foundations of applying the approach of empathy in poetry translation are narrated. In Chapter Four, a comparison of aesthetic empathy between the two English versions of poetry in *Hongloumeng* is made. Firstly, it is a brief introduction to poetry in *Hongloumeng* and its two English translated versions. In addition, a comparison of aesthetic empathy from the perspective of sense, sound and form is made respectively. In Chapter Five, a comparison of cultural empathy between the two English versions of poetry in *Hongloumeng* is made, in terms of ecology, material, society, religion and linguistics respectively. In Chapter Six, a comparison of pragmatic empathy between the two English versions of poetry in *Hongloumeng* is made, from the angle of pragma-linguistic empathy and socio-pragmatic empathy. After the careful comparison, it can be seen that Yang mainly empathizes towards the author and the ST while Hawkes mainly empathizes towards the readers and the TT. Chapter Seven puts forward possible explanations for these two different empathetic approaches.

Chapter One
Literature Review

Empathy has been a hot topic in linguistics for centuries and was noticed long before in ancient times both in China and the West, and as an artistic means, empathy has been practiced widely in Western artistic creations, and theories related to it have existed since Plato (437BC—347BC) and Aristotle (384BC—322BC). The present thesis is an attempt to study empathy in the masterpiece *Hongloumeng*. This chapter will be an introduction of some notions related to empathy: its definition, development and the difference between Chinese and the Western empathy. Then a review will be made of the related theses and papers on poetry translation in *Hongloumeng*.

1.1 Definition of empathy

1.1.1 Origin of empathy

The contemporary notion *empathy* was derived from the German word *Einfühlung*, which originally meant "feeling into" (Goldstein and Michaels, 1985), and the tendency of observers to project themselves into what they observed, typically some physical objects of beauty. (Davis, 1996)

In the late nineteenth century, the concept of *Einfühlung*, as "feeling into", was proposed by Rudolph Lotz (1817—1881) and Wilhelm Wundt (1832—1920). Later Friedrich Theodore Vischer (1807—1887), a German aesthetician, understood as "reflecting or feeling into", and regarded *Einfühlung* as "the aesthetic symbolic function".

In 1897, another German aesthetician Theodore Lipps (1851—1914) introduced the term *Einfühlung* as it was formulated by Robert Vischer in his writings about aesthetic perception and appreciation. In examining and contemplating an object (of art, nature, etc.), Lipps believed one projected oneself into the object (e. g., "feeling together with"), established an identification between it and oneself, engaged in a process of inner imitation, and in this manner came more fully to understand and appreciate it. Some years later, Lipps (1926) extended this definitional position to include people and not only objects as the targets of empathic efforts. (quoted in Goldstein and Michaels, 1985: 4) Johannes Volkelt (1848—1930) stated like Lipps the structure of aesthetic consciousness, with the concept of empathy as his focus. He quoted a basic concept in epistemology, the concept of certitude, and considered the certitude for the other self as the foundation of empathy. Karl Groos (1861—1946), also a German aesthetician, whose basic thoughts were similar to empathy, regulated the nucleus of aesthetically appreciative experiences in inner imitation. In these representatives' opinions, the term

Einfühlung described the projection of a sense of the inward feeling of our bodily state into inanimate objects.

The original word in German *Einfühlung* was later translated as empathy in American experimental psychology by Tichener in the early twentieth century, and eventually shifted the emphasis from internal acts to content. Tichener thought that "one could not know about the consciousness of another person by reasoning analogically from one's own mental processes to those of another. One could do this only by inner imitation." (quoted in Eisenberg and Strayer, 1987: 20) He later changed the notion of empathy from an amalgamation of visual and muscular imagery to a feeling, or projecting of one's self into an object, and therefore, it became a way to humanize our surroundings. Both Lipps and Tichener believed that empathy was an inner imitation, and argued that "witnessing another's emotional state prompts the observer to covertly, internally, imitate the other's emotional cues." (Davis, 1996: 5) This affective sharing of emotions between target and observer was said to foster a better understanding in social context, and easy to see that both Lipps and Titchener defined empathy in affective ways, the sharing of affect is a primary component.

Contrarily, a French aesthetician Victor Basch (1865—1944) thought that empathy was just "aesthetic sympathy", that is, to give inanimate things lives, personification and vitality and empathize and resonate with these things, because sympathy was just separating with the self, endowing and infusing the other things with the self. Vernon Lee (1856—1935) in Britain concluded that empathy was to transfer the general concepts consisting of the averaging and fundamental traces of memory to the object. She believed that empathy was not to transfer the subject's feelings directly to the object like what its name indicated. The main feature of her theory in its earlier formulations was the great stress upon the importance of organic sensations and bodily posture. In her opinion, "What we project into the object... is mainly the emotions and ideas of which the organic mimicry and bodily accommodations are the symptoms." In the account here reprinted, she differs from Lipps in one important respect. She objects to the conception of empathy "as a metaphysical and quasi-mythological projection of the ego into the object or shape under consideration." (Rader, 1960: 368)

All the above-mentioned representatives believe that witnessing another's emotional state prompts the observer covertly and internally to imitate the other's emotional cues. (Davis, 1996: 5) In the empathetic process, people view things as if they were in the same environment with these things, and the things seem to have feelings, thoughts, sentiments, wills and activities. At the same time, people themselves will be affected by such imaginary feelings and then come to resonate and sympathize with these things. So, traditionally empathy involves sharing the perceived emotion of another — "feeling with" another. This vicarious affective reaction may occur as a response to overt perceptible cues indicative of another's affective state (e. g., a person's facial expressions), or as the consequence of inferring another's state on the basis of indirect cues (e. g., the nature of the other's situation). This emotional sharing of sentiments between targets and observers can foster a better understanding in social context.

1.1.2 Cognitive elements in empathy

Later, several other contributors such as George Mead, Lauren Wispé, Kohler departed from the traditional general view of affective responses, such as, inner imitation, sharing of emotions, or emotional reactions, and put greater emphasis on deliberate cognitive process and apprehension in a purely cognitive capacity like perception and understanding. "Cognitive empathy emerges a further step, in which there is recognition of the other's experience as belonging to the other, without losing the distinction between self and other in emotional projection. These emotions require certain cognitive abilities and a well-developed sense of self." (秦希仁, 2007: 9)

From a cognitive perspective, empathy consists of either understanding the psychology of others (i. e., their thoughts, intentions, feelings, etc.) or, more specifically, their feelings. In either case, the processes responsible for such understanding are cognitive. Cognitive empathy has been defined as the ability to cognitively understand situations from another person's perspective (Hogan, 1969), just as the definition of empathy in *The Encyclopedia Britannica* (1999 edition) "The ability to imagine oneself in another's place and understand the other's feelings, desires, ideas, and actions. It is a term coined in the early 20th century, equivalent to the German *Einfühlung*. The term is used with special (but not exclusive) reference to aesthetic experience. The most obvious example, perhaps, is that of the actor or singer who genuinely feels the part he is performing. With other works of arts, a spectator may, by a kind of introjections, feel himself involved in what he observes or contemplates. The use of empathy is an important part of the counseling technique developed by the American psychologist Carl Rogers.

Kohler was one of the first advocates to argue in a more cognitive vein. Rather than going on to concentrate on "feeling into" the experiences of another, Kohler holds that empathy is more the understanding of other's feelings that sharing of them. One connotation of his view is that "understanding other people could be accomplished merely by viewing and interpreting the actor's actions, movements, and physical cues. Processes leading to affective sharing were no longer essential." (Davis, 1996: 6) At roughly the same time, Mead (1934), who recognized the self-other differentiation in empathy, added a cognitive component, an ability to understand, to empathy. He defined empathy as

"Empathy is the capacity to take the role of the other and to adopt alternative perspectives vis-à-vis oneself," (Mead, 1934: 27) which is from a psychological perspective, and emphasizes a person's ability of role exchanges.

Lauren Wispé views empathy in more cognitive terms than the other contributors do, and he defined empathy as the following: "Empathy refers to the attempt by one self-aware self to comprehend unjudgmentally the positive and negative experiences of another self. These emotions and reactions are often unclearly understood by the other person...so one important aspect of the process is empathic accuracy inasmuch as the purpose of empathy is often (but not necessarily) to provide understanding for one or both parties. Empathy depends upon the use of imaginal and mimetic capabilities and it is most often an effortful process." (Eisenberg and Strayer, 1987: 4) For Wispé, empathy is a more active, effortful process in which the observers try to understand the target by deliberately "reaching out" to the other. (Davis, 1996: 8)

1.1.3 Affective elements in empathy

Empathy did not become truly popular within psychology until the work of Carl Rogers and Heinz Kohut who incorporated both affective and cognitive definitions of empathy by stating that being empathic is the ability to perceive another person's internal frame of reference with accuracy and with the affective components as if the responder were the person without ever losing oneself. Rogers offered two different definitions of empathy at different times. In 1959, he regarded empathy as a process and means "to perceive the internal frame of reference of another with accuracy and with the emotional components and meanings which pertain thereto as if one were the person, but without ever losing the 'as if' conditions." (quoted in Eisenberg and Strayer, 1987: 28) Thus, it means to sense the hurt or the pleasure of another as he senses it and to perceive the causes thereof as he perceives them, but without ever losing the recognition that it is as if I were hurt or pleased and so forth. More than ten years later, he (1975) defined empathy as a "process" rather than a state and that it means "entering the private perceptual world of the other and becoming thoroughly at home in it. It involves being sensitive... to the changing felt meanings which flow in this other person... It means temporarily living in his / her life. Moving about in it delicately without making judgments... It includes communicating your sensing of his/her world as you look with fresh and unfrightened eyes at elements of which the individual is fearful. It means frequently checking with him/her as to the accuracy of your sensings, and being guided by the responses you receive..." (quoted in Eisenberg and Strayer, 1987: 28) Rogers (1975) held it's likely that his later definition is the most complete and insightful description of empathy to date. Although the description is long, perhaps empathy is too complex a phenomenon for a short definition, so his definition of empathy is lengthy. (quoted in Eisenberg and Strayer, 1987: 28) Kohut defines empathy at two different levels, one being more abstract and the other more clinically applied. At the most abstract level, Kohut (1959) views empathy as "vicarious introspection." (quoted in Eisenberg and Strayer, 1987: 29) In a more applied definition Kohut states that empathy is for the "acquisition of objective knowledge about the inner life of another person." (quoted in Eisenberg and Strayer, 1987: 30) He even holds that empathy is the basis of all human interaction.

Carolyn Shantz (1983) described the affective component of empathy as "the emotional response of the self to, or with, the other's affect."(quoted in Goldstein and Michaels, 1985: 33) The affective focus on empathic content and process was conveyed by Hoffman (1976), who stated that "empathy refers to the involuntary, at times forceful, experiencing of another person's emotional state. It is elicited either by expressive cues which directly reflect the other's feelings or by other cues which convey the impact of external events on him." (quoted in Eisenberg and Strayer, 1987: 226) For Hoffman (1977) it is important that "(a) affect is aroused in the observer and (b) that quality and direction of the affect correspond sufficiently to that experienced by the model to warrant calling it a vicarious response." (quoted in Goldstein and Michaels, 1985: 33) Reik defined empathy as shared affect and proposed four phases of the empathy process. This process was described as moving from:

(1) an instinctive imitative activity and relaxation of conscious controls upon becoming absorbed by the object of empathy, through

(2) introjection of the other person into ourselves, and the consequent

(3) "reverberation" or "resonance" between the internalized feelings of the other and evocations of our own experience and imagination, to

(4) deliberate withdrawal and psychological distancing in order to effect clear differentiation of self and other person in the final phase. (quoted in Eisenberg and Strayer, 1987: 226)

1.1.4 Communicative elements in empathy

Beyond this joint affective and cognitive focus, a new kind of component has been identified and added to the definitions of empathy — communicative element. Empathy is a kind of prosocial behavior and contributes to social coherence. On the one hand, the ability to empathize facilitates communication. If we empathize properly when communicating with others, we make our partners comfortable and therefore make the communication a success. On the other hand, to empathize, we need to detect and describe our feelings and understandings. Without successful communication, empathy is covert and can't reach our partners. It is at the root of meaningful and deep communication. Recognizing the ability to convey and interpret emotions accurately is a further step to the understanding of empathy.

According to Stewart (1983), the empathetic process covers decentering, perception checking, and an emphasis on "the productive, creative quality of communication". (Stewart, 1983: 389) She advocates interpretive listening, which focuses on communicative action instead of internal psychological states, and the collective building of subjective understanding, rather than the transference of one person's thoughts to another; that's to say, the act of empathizing involves not only the ability to sensitively comprehend the other's affective world, but also to accurately and sensitively communicate this understanding to the target other; that is, empathy for these persons involves "communicating your sensing", "detecting and describing" and "facility in communicating this affective understanding." (quoted in Goldstein and Michaels, 1985: 5)

While different definitions mentioned above exist, three main "components" of empathy are routinely cited: affective, cognitive, and communicative. (Duan and Hill, 1996) Keefe offered a comprehensive definition aiming at reconciling the affective-cognitive-communicative feature of empathy. He suggested four phases of the empathic communicative process: "perceiving accurately the client's gestalt, allowing a direct feeling response to arise, holding, qualifying or distorting cognitive processes in abeyance, and separating his own feelings from those shared with the client." (quoted in Goldstein and Michaels, 1985: 6) Macarov (1978) observes that empathy has three contemporaneous meanings. Consistent with Keefe and others, our more comprehensive affective-cognitive-communicative stance is that empathy is optimally defined by all three of these meanings combined: (1) Taking the role of the other, viewing the world as he or she sees it, and experiencing his or her feelings. (2) Being adept at reading nonverbal communication and interpreting the feelings underlying it. (3) Giving off a feeling of caring, or sincerely trying to understand in a nonjudgmental or helping way. (quoted in Goldstein and Michaels, 1985: 7)

According to the definition of empathy, it can be concluded that: (1) Empathy consists of an affective component, a cognitive component and a communicative component, but researchers vary in the importance they concede to each of these components; (2) There is a tendency of integrating the three components.

Despite the differences in understanding empathy, there is a general consensus on what empathy is. It is made up of two processes: First, putting yourself into someone else's shoe, that is, understanding the other person, and second, understanding yourself, that is, an awareness and knowledge of your own feelings. In other words, “you can’t fully empathize — or know someone else — until you adequately know yourself.” (Brown, 1987: 107)

To sum up, “empathy” refers to taking another’s perspective so as to feel and understand what’s in others’ minds by means of communication, which can in turn make communication smooth and successful.

1.1.5 Empathy vs. Sympathy

Empathy is quite different from sympathy. The concept of sympathy has a long history while the term empathy is quite recent.

First as M. F. Basch (1983) has noted, in the Greek derivation, the prefix “em-” means “in” or “within”, while the prefix “sym-” means “with”, “along with” or “together”. Thus the term sympathy means “feeling with”, referring to sharing an experience, especially suffering with someone else while empathy means “feeling into”, signifying the ability to share feelings and understand another person’s feelings and thoughts.

Sympathy, as Ehmann (1971) observes, contains major elements of condolence, pity, and/ or agreement, none of which characterize empathy. (quoted in Goldstein and Michaels, 1985: 7) With regard to constituent processes, Buchheimer’s (1963) differentiation of sympathy from empathy re-emphasizes the temporary “merging into” stage of the empathic (but not sympathetic) process. (quoted in Goldstein and Michaels, 1985: 7) Katz (1963) makes much the same distinction. Empathy, he holds, focuses our attention on the feelings and context of the other person. Sympathy, in contrast, is a heightened attention to one's own feelings and the assumed similarity between such feelings and those of the person who is the stimulus for it. (quoted in Goldstein and Michaels, 1985: 7) He states (Katz, 1963) that "When we empathize, we lose ourselves in the new identity we have temporarily assumed. When we sympathize, we remain more conscious of our separate identity." (quoted in Goldstein and Michaels, 1985: 8)

1.2 A comparison between Chinese and Western empathy

It turns out to be true that empathy as a mutual psychological phenomenon and an aesthetic appreciation, has been widely practiced in the artistic creations and theories both in China and the West. But ancient Chinese empathy was far different from that in the West due to the discrepancy in its philosophical foundations, literature and art. The major advocates of Western empathy like Lipps, Croos and Vernon Lee all regard aesthetics as a science and construct relatively systematic theories from the perspective of beauty appreciation on the basis of the empathy phenomenon in aesthetic activities. For example, Lipps thinks that aesthetics is a subject of psychology, aesthetic empathy is actually a kind of aesthetic appreciation which is made up of interactive aesthetic objects and aesthetic subjects. But in China, empathy in artistic creation is more highlighted, so it has been applied to critical works on poetry, prose, academic comments and other artistic creations, in which it can be found that ancient Chinese empathy concepts have much in common with those in the West, in addition, they carry more profound connotations and are more dialectic than those in the West. "The common points from the angle of aesthetic appreciation or artistic creation are that both Chinese and Western empathy agree that empathizing is what human sentiments feel into and project into the external things and empathy is a sort of communication between sentiments and objects. The reason that empathy in China is richer in connotation is that the concept of empathy in Chinese classical aesthetics refers to not only empathizing with objects and mingling of objects and the self, but also empathizing with another person, which is not involved in the Western empathy, so empathy in Chinese aesthetics is often called empathizing with another person." (罗显克, 1999: 34. The translation is mine.) Thus, it can be seen that the empathy concept in China and the West is similar to each other and somehow different as well.

As for the constitution of aesthetic empathy or the features of empathy, empathy in China as well as the West puts emphasis on the following (罗显克, 1999: 35-38. The translation is mine.):

Firstly, there must be an object in aesthetic appreciation. Secondly, there must be a subject in it, too, and empathy in China and the West stresses its concern with the function of the subject. For the present, the function of the subject has been paid more and more attention to in aesthetic research. What's more, what's different from Western empathy is that in Chinese empathy the subject and the object are always well balanced, but the Western empathy tends to over-emphasize the function of the subject. Thirdly, the subject and the object should be unified instead of opposite, and both of them are supposed to keep the relationship of aesthetics. In Western empathy research, though Lipps' psychological explanation diverges in the problem of the empathy function from Croos' and Vernon Lee's, they all agree that the subject exists in the object, and the object is animated by the subject and embodies the unifying relationship of human lives, thoughts, feelings and will. Chinese empathy approaches not only emphasize that the empathy of the subject is realized by the object, but also emphasize the subject's feeling projected into the object.

As has been said above, there exist similarities as well as differences between Chinese and Western empathy concepts. The major differences are listed in the following aspects: their different connotations in sentiments and their different empathizing manners, which can be known from the fact that the Western empathy theorists believe that man is the center and nature is controlled and dominated by man, the object and the self are unequal, and the life and sentiments of the object are caused by empathy. That's to say, "in the West, the sentiment refers to human's lives, personalities, and his entire spirit, and the empathizing mode is mainly reflected by unidirectional orientation from the self to the things; on the contrary, in China the sentiment refers to different concrete emotional attitudes that are certain emotional characters that human has on objects, and empathy is the equation between the subject and the object and their mutual influence and dependence."

Whether from the Chinese empathy approach or the Western one, it can be concluded that only when a translator puts himself into others' shoes and projects personal aesthetical experience and perception into the original, can his translated version be successful.

1.3 Previous studies on poetry translation in *Hongloumeng*

With the rising status of China and increase of cross-cultural communication in the new era, ancient Chinese literature and culture have been paid more and more attention to by more and more westerners. *Hongloumeng*, as a masterpiece of classical Chinese novels, has won great popularity since its first appearance in the 1790s. In recent years, there have been a number of domestic researchers carrying out relevant studies on poetry translation in *Hongloumeng*. In this section, a brief introduction of related theses and papers on poetry translation in *Hongloumeng* will be made. These theses and papers have contributed a lot to the analysis of poetry translation in *Hongloumeng*. Articles in core academic journals and MA dissertations from the database of CNKI from 1994 to 2010 concerning poetry translation in *Hongloumeng* are searched and surveyed from varying perspectives, which is briefly presented in the following figure.

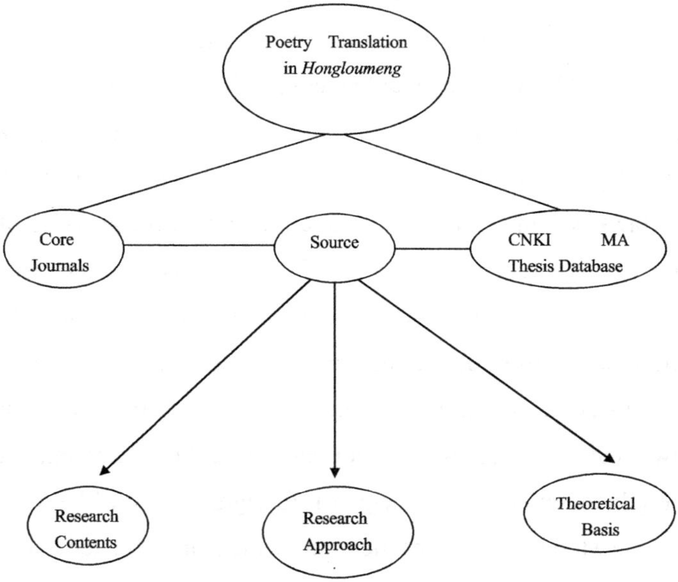

Figure 1.1 Poetry Translation in *Hongloumeng*

1.3.1 Research contents

It can be seen that most of the previous researches on poetry translation in *Hongloumeng* are confined to the micro perspective. Research is mostly carried out on specific items, concentrating on the discussion of translation methods and translation criteria, the comparative studies of different translated versions and the translator's subjectivity to probe into its translation. For example, Xu Jiachang (1996) studied the features of poetry in *Hongloumeng*, and it leads the way to its translation. As time goes on, the study on it is becoming more and more popular. Zhu Xiaoxi (1997) made a detailed comparison of two versions of poetry translation in *Hongloumeng*. Based on the comparative study of poetry in the English versions of *Hongloumeng* by Yang and Hawkes, Liu Man (2006) made a comparative analysis of the different translation strategies of the poetry in the English versions adopted by them respectively and discussed the operational factors influencing their strategies in accordance with the translation of cultural content of the poetry. The analysis shows that in the course of rendering the cultural elements, Yang generally adopted the strategy of foreignization, while Hawkes used the strategy of domestication, which are affected basically by four types of factors. Chen Yan (2007) made a brief study on the translator's subjective ideology in poetry translation in *Hongloumeng*. From the illustration with the examples from the two different versions of *Hongloumeng*, it can be concluded that the translator's subjectivity is undoubtedly manifested in the whole process of translation, and is determined by his purpose of translation and culture orientation. Luo Jing (2010) carried out a comparative study of the two versions of the translation of poetry in *Hongloumeng*. Through case studies it can be seen that Yang, regarding preserving and introducing Chinese heritage as his purpose, adopted a more semantic and source-culture-oriented translation; while Hawkes, with a purpose of pleasing the target reader, adopted a communicative and target-culture-oriented translation. At last his analysis leads to the conclusion that both semantic translation and communicative translation have their advantages and drawbacks. Neither of them alone can fulfill the translation task; the principle of translation should be relative and polysynthetic, but not absolute. Only when translators take advantages of both translation methods, can they reproduce the cultural connotation of *Hongloumeng*, achieve the goal of cultural communication between China and Western countries simultaneously.

1.3.2 Research approaches

Generally speaking, research approaches can be divided into two categories, that is, Linguistic Approach and Cultural Approach.

Linguistic Approach means that research is implemented

from the angle of linguistic theory. Fuzzy Linguistics, Cognitive Linguistics and Systemic Functional Linguistics are common approaches adopted to the study of poetry translation in *Hongloumeng*. For example, Ma Na (2005) made an attempt to analyze the English versions of Yang Xianyi and Hawkes, from the perspective of the metafunction theory of Systemic Functional Linguistics. By following the introduction of the theoretical claims of Systemic Functional Linguistics, the paper has carried out the analysis from three aspects, i.e. the ideational function, the interpersonal function and the textual function, so as to help the researchers rehandle the problems occurring in the process of translation, especially for poetry translation. Moreover, the practicality and operability of Systemic Functional Linguistics applied in the study of poetry translation can be checked out by means of such an analysis. Cao Jianhui (2009) made great efforts to study the specific strategies in translating fuzziness and illustrated with examples from three levels—linguistics, rhetoric and culture in the poems of *Hongloumeng* from the perspective of fuzzy linguistics.

Cultural Approach means that studies are conducted with the appliance of culture, concerning Post-colonisim, Feminism and Inter-textuality, etc. For instance, Wang Wei (2008) chose the translation of inter-textual signs in the poems of *Hongloumeng* as research subjects and summarized that full consideration of inter-textuality in translation could help the translator effectively overcome the huge cultural obstacles and achieve more successful cultural exchange. This is further confirmed by the brief criticism on the two English versions of *Hongloumeng*, thus verifying the importance of inter-textuality in translation and the conveyance of cultural connotations.

1.3.3 Theoretical basis

In terms of the theoretical basis of the research and studies on poetry translation in *Hongloumeng*, theories such as Reception Aesthetics, Skopostheorie, Relevance Theory, Aesthetic Empathy and Hermeneutics and so on have been frequently utilized. For instance, Sun Wenxia (2004) with the application of Liu Miqing's theory of stylistic translation, has tried to make a tentative study on the style transference in poetry translation in *Hongloumeng* from the angles of a stylistic formal markers and non-formal markers. Zhang Weiping (2009) studied the origin of pragmatic empathy, and analyzed the empathic reasons of the two different translators and also compared their different strategies in translating the poetry in *Hongloumeng* from the angle of pragmatic empathy. He concluded that Yang tends to translate semantically to empathize between the author and the source text, leaving the author in peace as much as possible, and move the reader towards him. On the contrary, Hawkes used the communicative translation strategy on the whole and empathized between the reader and the target text, leaving the reader in peace as much as possible, and moved the author towards him.

Zhu Huifen (2007) in her thesis *A Comparative Study of Two English Versions of Poems in the Story of the Stone from the Angle of Reception Aesthetics* attempted to study the aesthetic affects of the translation of the poems in the novel of *Hongloumeng* in order to solve the problem of preserving the aesthetic effects of Chinese poems in translation and keep the target texts acceptable to the target language readers form the aspects of beauty of verses, form, sense and flavor and meanwhile ensure the acceptability of the translated versions to target readers. Zhang Yan (2007) in *On Poetry Translation in Hongloumeng from the Perspective of Skopostheorie* attempted to apply Skopostheorie to poetry translation in *Hongloumeng*, adopting the two English versions by Yang and Hawkes for case study. At the end of the thesis, an conclusion is drawn that Yang adopted foreignization regarding preserving and introducing Chinese cultural heritage as his purpose, while Hawkes adopted domestication with the purpose of pleasing target readers. Qin Xiren (2007) in *A Comparative Study on the Two English Translations of Lin Daiyu's Poetry: an Empathetic Perspective* chose some of the poems composed by Lin Daiyu, doing a comparative study between Yang's and Hawkes' poetry translation from the perspective of empathy, in order to exemplify how the translators of these two translations empathize with the poets of the original in poetry translation under the guidance of empathy theory.

We can see from the above introduction, poetry translation has been studied from different angles at the early stage. But in terms of research approaches, most researchers employ the methodologies in traditional prescriptive translation studies, neglecting the historical, social, cultural, individual and subjective factors. Besides, pure comparative study among different translated versions is widely utilized, concentrating on the evaluation, assessment and comparison of the translated versions. Though various theses and papers on the poetry in *Hongloumeng* have been written, studies with regard to possible explanations for different empathetic approaches and their theoretical basis-empathy are rare. This thesis attempts to combine the two, the study of different translation approaches from the view of empathy to investigate the possible explanations for Yang's and Hawkes' different empathetic approaches.

Chapter Two
Poetry and Poetry Translation

In the 20th century, the palmy time for translation, empathy was introduced into translation theories. As is well known, poetry is the most subtle and delicate type of literature. It is the natural overflow of human emotions. The success or failure of a translation relies on whether the translator has aroused similar aesthetic and emotional experiences in target language readers. In what follows, some basic notions of poetry, including its definition, features and the basic elements of poetry will be discussed.

2.1 The definition of poetry

Poetry, as one of the highest representative form of literature, has something to do with the poet's creative thinking such as inspiration, imagination and intuition, and it is also an imaginative awareness of experience expressed through meaning, sound, and rhythmic language choices in order to evoke an emotional response. It is deemed as a tool to convey pleasure and sorrow, to delight our ear, mind and soul and to satisfy our crave for beauty and music through the power of language. Poetry is language in its most condensed and refined expression, in which the language is predominantly equivocal, ambiguous and connotative rather than clear, direct and denotative. At the same time, as an ancient form it has gone through numerous and drastic reinventions over time. Ever since its emergency, many researchers have been searching for an accurate definition of poetry, but there is not a unified description or formula. Different researchers have different definitions and understanding of poetry. Willian Wordsworth pointed that all poetry is the spontaneous overflow of powerful feeling; (quoted in Abrams, 1999: 242) Ebenezer Elliott looked on poetry as "impassioned truth" ; (quoted in Abrams, 1999: 1142) and in Dickinson's opinion, "If I read a book and it makes my body so cold no fire ever can warm me, I know that is poetry. If I feel physically as if the top of my head were taken off I know that is poetry."; (quoted in 米云辉, 2004: 1. The translation is mine) Newmark states that "poetry represents the thing in order to convey the feeling in particular, and however concrete the language, each represents something else-a feeling, a behavior, a view of life as well as itself." (Newmark, 2001: 164) Whatever the definition, the soul of poetry lies in the use of language in a figurative, metaphorical mode of expression that transcends traditional semantic limitations of language.

From the above definitions of poetry, the conclusion can be drawn that poetry, universal to all people, in all places and at all times, is a highly condensed form of literature, and is meant to express the subtle and complex feelings, interpret our hidden emotions and create special art effects. Thus, poetry translation requires not only the transference of linguistic units, but also transformation of the artistic beauty and spirit. In other words, painstaking efforts are needed in translating such a literary genre that has the most concise way to convey the experience of human beings.

2.2 The three basic elements of poetry

Poems call for the beauty in form, sound and meaning. (刘重德, 2003: 129) Therefore, there are three basic elements of poetry: sound, form and meaning.

2.2.1 Sound

Poetry is defined as "musical thought" by Thomas Carlyle, for it has not only strong rhythm but also poetic medoly, which makes poetry distinctive from prose.

Rhythm refers to the passage of regular or approximately equivalent time intervals between definite events or the recurrence of specific sounds or kinds of sounds or the recurrence of stressed and unstressed syllables. (戴继国, 2005: 5) A single line of a poem is called a verse. In each verse, the order of stressed and unstressed syllables usually occurs repeatedly so as to produce a music-like pattern. This pattern is called rhythm, the same as a beat in music.

Rhythmic pattern is one of the most important characteristics in prosody. In real life, we can say the rhythmic pattern is the core in language. In poetry, the accompaniment of rhythmic pattern gives both pleasure and emotional response to listeners or readers, for it establishes a pattern of expectations and rewards the listeners or readers with the pleasure of a series of fulfillment of gratifications.

Rhyme scheme is the most obvious characteristic of a poem. Rhyme is the repetition of the stressed vowel sound and all succeeding sounds. In detail, it means close similarity or identity of sound between syllables occupying corresponding positions in two or more lines or verse, which is more than a mere ornament or device of versification, for it performs valuable functions in helping the poet to emphasize something, expressing special feelings and intensifying the significance of the rhymed words. There are generally two kinds of rhymes: internal rhyme and end rhyme. Internal rhyme is the repetition of the same or similar sounds occurring within a line, while end rhyme means the repetition of the same or similar sounds of the ending words of lines occurring between or among lines.

2.2.2 Form

The form of a literary work, according to Kirszner and Mandell (1997: 827), usually refers to "its structure or shape, the way its parts fit together to form a whole; poetic form is the design of a poem described in terms of rhyme, meter and stanzaic pattern." In English, there are two kinds of forms about poem: closed form and open form. A poem written in closed form is characterized by regular patterns of meter, rhyme, line length, and stanzaic divisions. An open form poem makes occasional use of rhyme and meter without conventional stanzaic pattern, consistent metrical pattern, or repeated rhyme scheme. Generally speaking, poetic form, consisting of the construction of lines, punctuations, and numbers of words and order of lines, is the carrier of content and information. People who are familiar with poetry can usually tell what the form of a poem is when they first look at it. The form tells the reader what to expect from the poem, and the person who writes the poem can "play" with the form in interesting ways.

2.2.3 Meaning

Poetry, as a kind of language use, has the fundamental function of transmitting information, in which human beings gibe rhythmic expressions to their most imaginative and intense perception of the world. In poetry, words and image are two major elements for expressing meaning,

As is known to all, words are the basic units of a language. In poetry, the abundance and diversity of word meaning are just what poets need when expressing rich feelings within such short lines.

Image, as a vehicle to convey experiences and express deep sentiments, is frequently employed in literature, especially in poetry. The poet collects all kind of materials such as mountains and lakes, flowers and trees, animals and birds, etc. from the society and nature around himself to draw a picture in his mind, and image is the mental picture formed in the poet's mind. Then the poet uses the poetic language to convey his experiences and express his touching, moving and deep sentiments.

The beauty in a poem lies not only in the words a poet employs but also in all the above-mentioned elements such as rhyme, tone, meter and sound.

2.3 Text types and translation emphases

It is necessary for a translator to realize what kind of texts he is translating because the method of translating a poem is quite different from that of translating a scientific text. The text typology is very important for a translator because different types of texts determine different language functions. For example, scientific and technological translations should be accurate in meaning or content as the first principle while literary texts have to be rendered to retain both their aesthetic values and the meaning of the original texts.

According to J. B. Casagrande, an American linguist, there are four groups of text types: (1) pragmatic, (2) aesthetic-artistic, (3) linguistic, and (4) ethnographic translations. Otto Kade, a

German linguist, pointed out that due to the very different characters of various types of texts, there is no single translation pattern or model that can be equally valid for them all. As we can see, they both hold identical views on the text types. Katharina Reiss said, “it is not only justifiable but also imperative to develop a typology of texts to meet the demands of both translating and objective translation critics.” (Reiss, 2004: 23) Therefore, Reiss divided the text type into four groups borrowing from Karl Buhler's three way categorization of the functions of language, the main characteristics of each text type summarized by Reiss can be seen in the following table.

Table 2.1

Functional characteristics of text types and links to translation methods

(adapted from Reiss 1971) (quoted in Munday, 2001: 74)

Text type	Informative	Expressive	Operative
Language	Informative	Expressive	Appellative
function	(representing objects and facts)	(expressing sender's attitude	(making an appeal to text receiver)
Language dimension	Logical	Aesthetic	Dialogic
Text focus	Content-focused	Form-focused	Appellative focused
TT should	Transmit referential content	Transmit aesthetic form	Elicit desired response
Translation method	‘Plain prose’ explicitation as required	‘Identifying’ method, adopt perspective of ST	Adaptive equivalent effect

Reiss' fourth text type is audiomedial text, which is not represented in the table. It supplements the other three functions with visual images, music, etc., such as films and visual and spoken advertisements. As is seen from the table, the function of language in the content-focused text (information, knowledge, opinions, etc.) is to represent; in the form-focused text (all the artistic literary work), to express; in the appeal-focused (advertisement, electoral speech, sermon, and so on), to persuade; in the audiomedial text (such as radio newcasts and reports, operating instructions), to speak. The emphasis in translating a content-focused text must be laid on its aesthetic forms; the appeal-focused text, its clear appeal to the hearer or reader of the text; and the audio-medial text, its graphic, acoustics, and visual kind of expression. According to Reiss, literary works were included in the form-focused text in which a translator "will not mimic slavishly (adopt) the forms of the source language, but rather appreciate the form of the source language and be inspired by it to discover an analogous form in the target language, one which will elicit a similar response in the reader." (Reiss, 2004: 33)

Reiss pays much attention to the form and stylistic characters of the source language in literary works and suggests specific translation methods according to text type. As a result, the TT of an expressive text should transmit the aesthetic and artistic form of the ST, and the emphasis in poetry translation should be laid on the aesthetic values of the source text. The translation should use the "identifying" method, with the translator adopting the standpoint of the ST author. A poetry translator should try to realize how the original writer expresses instead of what he states.

2.4 The translatability of poetry

Concerning the problem of translating poems, quite a few researchers have made studies both at home and abroad. Some think that poems are translatable and others don't think so, it is really a problem. The translatability of poetry has long been disputed in the area of translation study by writers and translators. No agreement has been reached so far.

Some scholars, thinkers, writers and even translators have struggled to define the difficulties of translating poetry, suspected and denied the translatability absolutely. In the West, statements to that effect are legion, from Dante, to Shelly, to Robert Frost, etc. Bonnyfoy (1989: 186) expresses his definite attitude towards this issue: "the answer to the question, 'Can one translate a poem? 'is of course no. The translator meets too many contradictions that he can't eliminate: he must make too many sacrifices." He further advocates that poetry is untranslatable unless the necessity compels a translator to translate a certain poem. There is always something implied beyond language. Nabokov points out that "the problem, then, is a choice between rhyme and rhythm: can a translation while rendering with fidelity absolute fidelity the whole text, and nothing but the text, keep the form of the original, its rhythm and its rhyme?" (quoted in Schulte and Biguenet, 1992: 1, 32) Poetry has different forms and structures in different cultures. The forms and structures of both Chinese and English poetry are so complicated that each has its unique system of rhyme, rhythm and so on. The content and form are inseparably linked in poetry. Owing to the cultural and linguistic difference, the forms in one language are difficult to transpose across languages. When it comes to poetry and its translation, Susan Bassnett adopts an even melancholy tone, "There are countless book-shelves, probably enough to fill entire libraries, of self-indulgent nonsense on poetry. In comparison with the quantity of poetry actually produced, the amount of redundant commentary must be at least double. A great deal of this literature claims that poetry is something apart, that the poet is possessed of some special essential quality that enables the creation of a superior type of text, the poem. And there is a great deal of nonsense written about poetry and translation too, of which probably the best known is Robert Frost's immensely silly remark that 'poetry is what gets lost in translation', which implies that poetry is some intangible, ineffable thing (a presence? a spirit?) which, although constructed in language cannot be transposed *across* languages." (Bassnett and Lefevere, 2004: 57) The famous British poet Shelley describes the difficulties of poetry translation like this in his *Defence of Poetry*,

"It were as wise to cast a violet into a crucible that you might discover the formal principles of its color and odor, as seek to transfuse from one language into another the creation of a poet. The plant must spring again from its seed, or it will bear no flower and this is the burthen of the curse of Babel." (quoted in Bassnett and Lefevere, 2004: 58)

In China, the translatability of poetry is likewise problematic, and the pessimistic viewpoint is just as prevalent. Even those poetry translators themselves believe that the translations of poetry often lose most of the original musical qualities and don't sufficiently create a sense of poetry. In the early 20s, Mao Dun said that a poem translated is the original retold and cannot be regarded as the original. Wen Yiduo concludes that a good Chinese poem defies translation, and if you insist on translating it, you can only ruin it. Wang Yizhu declares "Directly, I thought poetry is untranslatable. The reason is very simple. The verve and poetic imagery, namely, the flavor of poetry that is the essence of poetry, to a great extent, has melted into the language used by the poet, All of which can't be expressed in another language (or dialect)." (王以铸, 1984: 874. The translation is mine.)

Besides, some scholars attribute untranslatability to the differences in nature between source language and target language, related to linguistic differences and cultural differences. J. C. Catford (Catford, 1965: 93-99) took a strictly linguistic point of view and distinguished two types of untranslatability, which he terms linguistic untranslatability and cultural untranslatability. On the linguistic level, untranslatability occurs when there is no lexical or syntactical substitute in the target language for a source language item. Cultural untranslatability arises when a situational feature, functionally relevant for the source language text, is completely absent from the culture of which the target language is a part. Whorf came to the conclusion that "people who use languages with very different grammars are led by these grammars to typically different observations and different values for outwardly similar observations." (Whorf, 1958: 20) The principle of linguistic relativity has a substantial implication for translation, taken to its extreme, "the notion that language conditions thought and that both are inextricably bound up with the individual culture of the community that speaks the language concerned would mean that ultimate translation is impossible." (Snell-Hornby, 2001: 4)

I hold that it is possible, but quite difficult, to translate poems satisfactorily and successfully. Translatability refers to the degree of accuracy and equivalence in the process of translation rather than whether a language can be translated into another. During the translation process, unlimited translation activities are carried out, which have promoted the cultural exchange and shared the historical and cultural heritage among different countries, which proves that a language or literary work can be translated. As Baker said, "The translation of poetry is generally held to be the most difficult, demanding, and possibly rewarding form of translation. It has been the subject of a great deal of discussion, particularly within the field of LITERARY TRANSLATION, where far more has been written about the translation of poetry than about either prose or DRAMA. Much of the discussion consists of a theoretical questioning of the very possibility of poetry translation, even though its practice is universally accepted and has been for at least 2000 year, during which translated poetry has influenced and often become part of the canon of the TL poetic translation; Fitzgerald's *Rubaiyat of Omar Khayyam* (1859) and Pound's *Cantos* (1925) are obvious examples." (Baker, 1998: 170) As a result, despite the great linguistic and cultural obstacles, poetry is mostly susceptible to rendition. Though there do exist apparent differences among different languages, it can't be denied that there are more similarities than differences existing extensively among different languages. As Nida and Reyburn hold, "At first, one is almost inevitably impressed with the differences between cultures, but gradually one begins to see more and more similarities and to discover beneath the surface of the divergences many features that cultures have in common. These are essentially the universals or near universals of culture that make possible communication within and between languages." (Nida and Reyburn, 1981: 96) In Jiang Feng's opinion (江枫), poetry is a part of the cultural activities all over the world, and even if there exist great differences between different nations, some similarities among different nations construct the base on which poetry can be translated. It is obvious that there exists poetry or other language arts similar to poetry or songs in a nation or tribe. (许钧 , 2001: 113. The translation is mine.) Scholars admit the difficulty in translation practice but they still try to reproduce the unity of form and content of the original work. G. Mounin (1963) insisted that "it is the content of the poem and the relation between content and form as a whole that should be taken into consideration in the translation of poetry ... a translator should be able to convey the same content and produce the same or similar affect in the appropriate form of poetry in another language." (Chan and Pollard, 1995: 1065) From his idea, we can see that Mounin stands up for the translatability of poetry. Another scholar, Susan Bassnett also voiced a positive view on poetry translation when she wrote, "When the rewriter is perfectly fused with the source, a poem is translated. That this happens so frequently is a cause for celebration." (Bassnett and Lefevere, 2004: 74) On the basis of similarities of languages, translatability becomes possible. The following four reasons support my view on the translatability of poetry.

2.4.1 Language universals

Languages have much in common. Focusing on the

hierarchical structure of languages, Nida states in his article *Approaches to Translating in the Western World*, "all languages have a limited set of discreet sounds, have a hierarchical set of levels from the morpheme to the total discourse, employ all the major genres (for example, legends, history, stories, poetry, song, parables, personal accounts, laws, arguments, and conversation), consist of open systems for borrowing or making up words for new concepts, and employ figurative languages including both metaphors (based on likeness) and metonyms (based on associations)." (Nida, 1984: 15) Chomsky suggests that "in the deeper levels of linguistic structure languages will be found to share aspects of form that are a common human possession realized differently at the surface in different languages." (Robins, 1967: 126) The general similarities of language account for the foundation of the translatability, just as uniqueness of languages accounts for untranslatability or the degree of translatability.

2.4.2 Common physiological function and emotional response

Human beings as a unity face the world and are engaged in practical activities. Man's social being determines his social consciousness, and the objective world is mirrored into our brain. The content of thinking is constrained by the objective conditions which are independent of our consciousness. The world is consistent or similar to all nations no matter which language they speak, which leads to unanimous topics of thinking that is the reflection over the objective world by each nation, which, in turn, determines the generality of thinking. In short, all sorts of measures of value like the true, the good, the beautiful and the ugly apply to all nations. Thus for the above-mentioned reason of general characteristics, translation of poetry is possible. For example, we tend to associate the sea with broadness and the spirit of hard-working, when the images of "东临碣石，以观沧海"（曹操《步出夏门行·观沧海》）"欲穷千里目，更上一层楼"（王之涣《登鹳雀楼》）appear in our minds, they easily remind us of magnanimity and positive attitude with empathy towards the ST.

There exist many things common to all who have the same physiological functions and they respond in a similar way to specific outer environment. "For instance, they all have the thinking power to reason logically and the feelings to express joy or sorrow, love or hatred, and possess the same nature, world and universe no matter what races they may be. In other words, all human beings are endowed by nature with the same mind which has the same function so that they can commune with one another. As a consequence, poetry, a product of the mind, is understandable, enjoyable and translatable." (刘重德, 2003: 128) For example, the little match girl in the story of *The Little-Seller* who died of hunger and cold would surely arouse sympathy regardless of the nationality. The following examples show that people from different cultures may have the same emotional responses. For instance, friendship is highly appreciated and valued by all generations of mankind. Wang Bo (王勃) composed a well-known couplet: "海内存知己，天涯若比邻"(王勃《送杜少府之任蜀州》). The great English poet Lord George Gordon Byron wrote a similar couplet in the *Stanzas To the Po*: "But that which keepeth us apart is not / Distance, not depth of wave, nor space of earth." Consider another couplet by Du Fu (杜甫): "此曲只应天上有，人间能得几回闻"(杜甫《增花卿》). Shakespeare wrote in *The Tempest* "Where should this music be? i'the air, or the earth?" It also proves that poetic minds think alike. (李晓红，2007: 24)

Waard and Nida state, "in adjustment to the physical environment, in the organization of society, in dealing with crucial stages of life (birth, puberty, marriage and death), in the development of elaborate ritual and symbolism, and in a drive for aesthetic expression (whether in decorating masks or in refining poetic form), people are amazingly alike." (Waard and Nida, 1985: 57) So it is possible for people to understand each other and try to find the words and expressions in the TL, which bear the similar meaning or image and arouse the similar emotion so as to communicate with each other successfully. Consequently, poetry, a product of thoughts and feeling, is understandable, translatable and can be appreciated.

2.4.3 The support of translation theories

Since the 1960s, supporters of the universal translatability notions have been attempting to express their ideas on a scientific foundation. Some of the most prominent twentieth-century linguists have reached a general agreement that though translating poems satisfactorily and successfully is quite difficult, it is still possible, because in substance, everything in one language can be expressed in another language. In Nida's words, "..., as linguists and anthropologists have discovered, that which unites mankind is greater than that which divides." (Nida, 1964: 2) According to Susan Bassnett, in spite of the impossibility of translating a poem from one language to another, a poem can be transplanted, and the seed of the poem can be cast in new soil and a new plant can be developed. Moreover, disproving of Robert Frost's argument of "poetry is what gets lost in translation", she ironically refutes that "poetry is not what is lost in translation; it is rather what we gain through translation and translators." (Bassnett and Lefevere, 2004: 74) The English poet Wordsworth says that "in spite of difference of soil and climate, of language and manners, of law and customs, in spite of things silently gone out of mind, and things violently destroyed; the Poet binds together by passion and knowledge and vast empire of human society, as it is spread over the whole earth, and over all times." (quoted in 劳陇, 1987: 216-217) Other authors accept a universal translatability hypothesis. Wilss states that “everything can be expressed in every language, the translatability of a text is [...] guaranteed by the existence of universal categories in syntax, semantic, and the (natural) logic of experience. Should a translation nevertheless fail to measure up to the original in terms of quality, the reason will (normally) be not an insufficiency of syntactic and lexical inventories in that particular TL, but rather the limited ability of the translator in regard to text analysis?” (Wilss, 2001: 49)

2.4.4 The support of translation practice

During the over 2000-year history of translation practice, most texts, including poems with strong artistic flavors, have been translated successfully and accurately. As long as we have projected our body into the body of the original writer, feeling the mind, and emotion, etc., we are sure to evoke in our mind the resonance with the original. Meanwhile, a good command of the TL and its rhyme ensure the translatability of poetry will come true. Innumerable historical facts of translation have proved that poetry is translatable. “The translatability of poetry has already been demonstrated by quantities of historical facts. The poems written by the well-known poets in the world, such as William Shakespeare, John Milton, Percy Bysshe Shelley, Lord Byron of England, Henry Wadsworth Longfellow and Walt Whiteman of the United States of American, Voctor-Marie Hugo of France,

Johann Wolfgang von Geothe of Germany, Aleksander Sergeevich Pushkin of Russia, Sir Rabindranath Tagore of India, were translated into various languages long ago and a great number of them were well-done." (刘重德, 2003: 128-129) Many translators at home and abroad have successfully translated a large quantity of excellent classical Chinese poems into different languages. Because of the successful translation, people all over the world are familiar with many famous poets in ancient China such as Li Bai, Du Fu, Wang Wei and Meng Haoran. In addition, a considerable number of modern Chinese men of letters translated their classical poems into English and had them published as *An English Version of Tang Poems* by Cai Tinggan, *A New Translation of Three Hundred Tang Poems* by Xu Yuanchong, and so on.

So far as contemporary poems are concerned, we can also find lots of them translated either from a foreign language into Chinese or from Chinese into a foreign language. Poetry is not only translatable, but also the translated poetry can even influence the TL readers and its culture. After reading those translations, we have appreciated the beauty of these world-famous poems. Equipped with its great power, the poem arouses in our body the same responses as those intended by the original author. The popularity and fame of works throughout the world should be attributed to translation. Such objective facts have proved translatability forcefully. All the above opinions reveal that difficult as it is, poetry translation provides a perfect platform for the translator to give full play to his subjective initiative. Therefore, there are no universally applicable translation standards or criteria for the evaluation and practice of poetry translation. Thus poetry translation remains an intimidating enterprise for translators. It is, therefore, still in need of some scientific theories for guidance and support. And that's exactly what I intend to explore in this thesis.

2.5 Basic issues for poetry translation

2.5.1 Poetry translation criteria

Different types of text demand different translation criteria as shown in Chapter Two. Texts of a relatively objective style, such as texts of science and technology as well as legality, put great emphasis on the objectivity of translation and pursue unified, identical and definitude meanings, thus asking for translators' absolute loyalty to the source-language text. Translations of such texts should be accurate, while translations of literary texts have to prevent its aesthetic value from being detracted from the meaning of the original text. Poetry, a literary form which represents a perfect combination of both form and content, is always regarded as the most difficult to translate. More time has been devoted to investigating the problems of translating poetry than any other literary mode. According to Liu

Zhongde, "a translator of poems should not be satisfied with the mere conveying of the ideas in the original, but must strive for the reproduction of the original beauty. To achieve this, he ought to, first of all, retain the original meaning and artistic conception and secondly, do his best to make his translation bear a certain due form, rhythm, and rime when necessary. Owing to the differences in the characteristics of various languages, it is both impossible and unnecessary for the translator to render the original poems word for word. However, he has the responsibility to try in a thousand and one ways to overcome the difficulties and even the individual untranslatabilities which may arise from the different characteristics of the original and target languages. The translator is allowed to make up the loss in the meaning of some fore-going or following words somewhere within the whole poem. What's most important for him to do in translating a poetic work is to keep its original artistic conception and style." (刘重德, 2003: 129-130) Such criteria clearly show the vital role of the translator's subjectivity and empathy in poetry translation.

As one of the most influential poetry translators in contemporary China, Xu Yuanchong (2009: 6) put forward his criterion of Three Beauties on poetry translation in the preface to *300 Tang Poems* —"... that is, translation should be faithful to the original in word, in form and in sense, while the art school emphasizes beauty, that it, a translated verse should be as beautiful as the original in sense, in sound and in form." Being beautiful in sense refers to that in the process of translating a poem, the translator is supposed to translate not only the surface meaning of the poem, but also the deep sense of it. For Xu, the translation process will be relatively easy if both the content and form of the poem are kept harmonious. If the content is inconsistent with the form, priority should be given to the form in the translation process. In case that the original form covers a few different meanings, the most beautiful one should be selected during translation. Being beautiful in sound means that the translator should do his outmost to present rhyme, rhythm and metre of the original one. For instance, if the original one is rhymed, the translated version should also be rhymed. In addition, being beautiful in form refers to the layout of the lines, antithesis formed by lines matched in sound and sense, and repetition of words or lines. Xu points out that the being beautiful in sense is the most important one followed by being beautiful in sound and then being beautiful in form.

Peter Newmark proposes that “in most examples of poetry translation, the translator first decides to choose a TL poetic form (viz. sonnet, ballad, quatrain, blank verse, etc.) as close as possible to that of the SL. Although the rhyming scheme is part of the form, its precise order may have to be dropped. Secondly, he will reproduce the figurative meaning, the concrete images of the poem. Lastly the settings, the thought-words, often the various techniques of the sound-effect produce the individual impact." (Newmark, 2001: 165) "Whether a translator gives priority to content or manner, and, within manner, which aspect—metre, rhyme, sound, structure-is to have priority, must depend not only on the values of the particular poem, but also on the translator's theory of poetry. Therefore no general theory of poetic translation is possible and all a translation theorist can do is to draw attention to the variety of possibilities and point to successful practice, unless he rashly wants to incorporate his theory of translation into his own theory of poetry." (Newmark, 2001: 165-166)

2.5.2 Poetry translation strategies

As is listed above, different translators have their own methods and ideas on how to translate a poem. Based on their translation experience, many scholars summarize a variety of poetry translation strategies.

Andre Lefevere catalogues sevens different strategies in poetic translation, which go as follows:(quoted in Bassnett, 2005: 87)

(1) Phonemic translation, which attempts to reproduce the SL sound in the TL while at the same time producing an acceptable paraphrase of the sense. Lefevere comes to the conclusion that although this works moderate well in the translation of onomatopoeia, the overall result is clumsy and often devoid of sense altogether.

(2) Literal translation, where the emphasis on word-for-word

translation distorts the sense and the syntax of the original.

(3) Metrical translation, where the dominant criterion is the reproduction of the SL metre. Lefevere concludes that, like literal translation, this method concentrates on one aspect of the SL text at the expense of the text as a whole.

(4) Poetry into prose. Here Lefevere concludes that distortion of the sense, communicative value and syntax of the SL text results from this method, although not to the same extent as with the literal or metrical types of translation.

(5) Rhymed translation, where the translator ‘enters into a double bondage’ of metre and rhyme. Lefevere's conclusions here are particularly harsh, since he feels that the end product is merely a ‘caricature’ of Catullus.

(6) Blank verse translation. Again the restrictions imposed on the translator by the choice of structure are emphasized, although the greater accuracy and higher degree of literalness obtained are also noted.

(7) Interpretation. Under this heading, Lefevere discusses what he calls versions where the substance of the SL text is retained but the form is changed and imitations where the translator produces a poem of his own which has ‘only title and point of departure, if those, in common with the source text’.

James Holmes, a great translator of poetry across several languages and distinguished scholar of translation, puts forward a few poetry translation strategies. The first is “imetic form”—in this case the translator reproduces the form of the original in the target language. This can obviously only happen where there are similar formal conventions already in existence, so that the translator can use a form with which readers are already familiar. However, Holmes points out that since a verse form cannot exist outside language, "it follows that no form can be 'retained' by the translator" and no verse from can ever be completely identical across literary system. This means, therefore, that an illusion of formal sameness is maintained, while in actuality the target language readers are being simultaneously confronted with something that is both the same and different, i. e. that has a quality of "strangeness". Holmes suggests that this is the case with blank-verse translations of Shakespeare into German. The second strategy is called "analogical form" which involves a formal shift, he suggested that the translator determines what the function of the original form is and then seeks an equivalent in the target language. The most obvious example of this technique would be the translation of the French alexandrine into English blank verse and vice versa. The third strategy is defined as "content-derivative", or "organic form". In this process, the translator starts with the semantic material of the source text and allows it to shape itself. This is basically Eara Pound's strategy in the twentieth century, fuelled also by the development of free verse. Holmes' fourth category is described as "deviant or extraneous form". In this type of translation, the translator utilizes a new form that is not signaled in any way in the source text, either in form or content. (quoted in Bassnett and Lefevere, 2004: 62-63)

Ezra Pound, a prominent poet and translator, holds the view that the translator needs to read well, to be aware of what the source text is, to understand both its formal properties and its literary dynamic as well as its status in the source system, and then has to take into account the role that text may have in the target system. According to Pound, three kinds of poetry may be found in any literature, and each kind has its corresponding translation strategy. The first kind is "melopoeia" where words are surcharged with musical property that directs the shape of the meaning. This musical quality can be appreciated by "the foreigner with the sensitive ear", but cannot be translated, "except perhaps by divine accident or even half a line at a time". The second kind is "phanopoeia", he regards as the easiest to translate, for this involves the creation of images in language. The image was, of course, central to Pound's poetics, as his deliberate choice of the highly imagistic Japanese and Chinese verse forms as models demonstrates. The third kind "logopoeia", "the dance of the intellect among words" is deemed to be untranslatable. Pound suggests that the way to proceed is to determine the author's state of mind and start from there. (quoted in Bassnett and Lefevere, 2004: 64)

Chapter Three
Application of the Approach of Empathy in Poetry Translation

3.1 Difficulties of poetry translation

As the oldest and most primitive genre of literature, poetry distinguishes itself by refined and terse diction, refreshing images and symbols. Crowned as the highest and the most concise form of art, it conveys the most complex and profound human emotions in fewest words. Overwhelmed by the aesthetic value of classical Chinese poetry, countless scholars both at home and abroad have been gladly focusing on its translation, making great contribution to introducing this immortal heritage of Chinese culture to the rest of the world, which facilitates the cultural communication between the East and the West. However, poetry translation is in any case not an easy task; the truth is that it is the most complex and challenging task among all the literary translations. Poetry calls for the beauty in meaning, sound and form, so does poetry translation, which aims to reproduce the original beauty and keep the aesthetics in the translated version. The American poet Robert Frost even said, "Poetry is what gets lost in translation," (Bassnett and Lefevere, 2004: 57) which highlights the difficulties of poetry translation. It is said that poetry suffers in translation, and the reader suffers with it.

3.1.1 Difficulties caused by linguistic differences

3.1.1.1 A tone language vs. a stress-timed language

Chinese is a tone language, which emphasizes different tones, so tone patterns play a vital role in contrasting meaning of words. The four tones of Chinese characters have no perfect equivalence in English, which are characterized by level tone, rising tone, falling-rising tone, and falling tone, all of which equip Chinese poetry with a characteristic cadence. The four tones are divided into two categories, the *ping sheng* or the *level tone*, which is relatively tense, and *ze sheng* or *oblique tone*, which is relatively slack. Thus, Chinese poetry is featured not only by its sound low and high, up and down, but also by the contrast of long and short syllables, thus forming a harmonious unity of four tones and the balance in sentence structure. (李晓红, 2007: 20)

On the contrary, English is a stress-timed language, which has notable stressed or unstressed sounds. Its poetry is mainly made up of metric foot and rhyme. A foot can be composed of two or three syllables, one of which must be stressed. The regular patterns of stressed and unstressed syllables are called meters, and the number of the meters decides the verse length of the

Classical English Poetry. What's more, rhyme plays a role in the musicality of different poetic languages. Generally speaking, Chinese poetry is mostly rhymed at the end of a sentence; in English poetry, besides the form rhymed at the end of a line, there are also two other forms: head rhyme (e.g. "sweet" and "spring") and internal rhyme (e.g. "king" and "spring"). The regular fall and rise produce rhythm, then the combination of foot and meter gives birth to various kinds of rhythm, conveying different emotions and feelings. Rhythm can't part with meaning. The following《好了歌》in *Hongloumeng* will illustrate the difference of Chinese and English poetry:

Example 1:

ST:

好了歌

世人都晓神仙好,惟有功名忘不了!
古今将相在何方?荒冢一堆草没了。
世人都晓神仙好,只有金银忘不了!
终朝只恨聚无多,及到多时眼闭了。
世人都晓神仙好,只有姣妻忘不了!
君生日日说恩情,君死又随人去了。
世人都晓神仙好,只有儿孙忘不了!
痴心父母古来多,孝顺儿孙谁见了?

(《红楼梦》第一回)

TT1:

All Good Things Must End

"All men long to be immortals
Yet to riches and rank each aspires;
The great ones of old, where are they now?
Their graves are a mass of briars.

All men long to be immortals,
Yet silver and gold they prize
And grub for money all their lives
Till death seals up their eyes,
All men long to be immortals
Yet dote on the wives they've wed.
Who swear to love their husband evermore
But remarry as soon as he's dead.
All men long to be immortals
Yet with getting sons won't have done.
Although fond parents are legion,
Who ever saw a really filial son?

(Yang's translation)

TT2:

Won-Done Song

Men all know that salvation should be won,
But with ambition won't have done, have done.
Where are the famous ones of days gone by?

In grassy graves they lie now, every one.
Men all know that salvation should be won,
But with their riches won't have done, have done.
Each day they grumble they've not made enough.
When they've enough, it's goodnight everyone

Men all know that salvation should be won,
But with their loving wives they won't have done.
The darlings every day protest their love:
But once you're dead, they're off with another one.

Men all know that salvation should be won,
But with their children won't have done, have done.
Yet though of patents fond there is no lack,
Of grateful children saw I ne'er a one.

(*Hawkes' version*)

The original song takes the form of seven-word poem where there are four stanzas.. However in the strict sense, it is not a regulated verse whose language is plain and simple, which seems like a folk song. The sentence of "世人都晓神仙好，只有金银忘不了" turns up over and over again in the first two lines of each stanza. The rhyming pattern of AABA with "好(hao)" "了(liao)" and "了(liao)" in the first, second, and fourth line is standard. No pattern of "*ping*" or "*ze*" is followed in the whole poem.

In Hawkes' version, there are ten syllables in each line. Iambic tetrameters are used, which are equal to four pauses in the original version. Its rhyme is both natural and strict. In the first, second and fourth line the rhyming words "won, done, one" are a reproduction of the metrical feet and sense of "好", "了" and "了" of the source language. And the use of " won, done, one" solves the problem of translating the comment of the Daoist on "好" and "了" in the following text. The following feet in his version read smoothly and give the readers a pleasant feeling:

First stanza: won, done, one;
Second stanza: won, done, everyone;
Third stanza: won, done, one;
Fourth stanza: won, done, one.

Comparatively, Yang's translated version is rather concise. It is mainly composed in iambic trimesters and tetrameters combined. Its rhyme scheme differs from "好，了，了". It has the single sound /s/, /n/ and /d/ as the feet, and abcb, abdb, aefe, and aghg as the rhyme scheme, which is relatively less impressive than that of Hawkes' version in terms of rhyme. Though it sounds lively with various metrical meters, it fails to agree with "好，了，了" in the original, which increases the difficulty in translating the comments of the Daoist. It can be concluded that both versions use the form of metrical verse, despite the linguistic differences.

3.1.1.2 An ideographic language vs. a spelling

language

Chinese characters are ideographic writings, which are a combination of form, sound and meaning relying on pictograms or characters. However, the English language is a kind of spelling language that usually resorts to pronunciation and spelling to bring out the meaning of words.

The Chinese language being an ideographic language, each of its written signs gives more ideas of the meaning of the character than the sound. For this reason it is indeed a great pity that its beauty of image and sound is usually completely lost when Chinese is translated into English, which is an alphabetic writing system with words made up of letters without any connotative meaning, therefore it is so hard to render the following the words"涕,泣,江边"in the poem《探春判词》"清明涕泣江边望,千里东风一梦遥". These two lines with one side of a character "氵" well describe Tan Chun's sad mood and sorrowful fate standing by waving rivers parting her relatives, "氵" means (three drops of) water, is employed three times in one line to describe her homesickness she suffered from. The employment of the specific characters with the implied meaning within their forms can help the readers to feel Tan Chun's sorrow and tragic destiny. Cao Xueqin frequently used this skill throughout his novel. The following poem serves as another example:

凡鸟偏从末世来,都知爱慕此生才。

一从二令三人木，哭向金陵事更哀。(《红楼梦》第五回)

This poem is meant as a hint of Wang Xifeng's fate, in which the first two characters "凡" and "鸟" respectively referring to "earthly" and "bird", make the Chinese character "凤" meaning "phoenix", and referring indirectly to Wang Xifeng. And "人" and "木" can be joined to form the character of "休", meaning "be dismissed". "一从二令三人木" is acknowledged as the reflection of Wang Xifeng's life, meaning that she has experienced three stages in her life, first yielding to her husband Jia Lian, then managing the whole household and at last being ousted from her husband's family. Any Chinese reader of common sense is able to figure out whom this poem is written to, but the English versions fail to present the meaning of this part.

3.1.2 Difficulties caused by grammar differences

Grammar is a very important part of linguistic research, for it describes the rules which govern the construction of language. As Chinese and English belong to different language families and are rooted in different cultures, there exist significant differences between their use, which can't be ignored in the translation process.

English, being alphabetical language, concentrating on the relations between tenses, numbers and the like, belongs to the

Indo-European language while Chinese belongs to Sino-Tibetan language family, which, being ideogram, is not burdened with tenses, genders, moods, cases, or numbers and so on, as a result, it gives great elasticity to Chinese poems and enables the writer to concentrate on essentials and be as concise as possible, also at the same time, making translators at a loss to decide the tenses, genders or moods, etc. which tends to give rise to ambiguity. For example:

1. Differences in number markers

Example 2:

ST:

月窟仙人缝缟袂，秋闺怨女拭啼痕。

（《红楼梦》第三十七回）

TT1:

The goddess of the moon sews a white gown,

The maid's weeping in autumn chamber never ends; ...

(*Yang's translation*)

TT2:

Moon-maidens stitched them with white silken thread,

And virgins' tears the new-made flowers did spot, ...

(*Hawkes' translation*)

These two lines are taken from the poem *Intoning White Begonias* composed by Lin Daiyu. When using nouns in English, we have to indicate the "number" of things or people. The plural form of nouns in English is often marked by "-s", while Chinese has few such markers. So when translating the two lines into English, the translators first should make sure how many "xianren" and "yuannv" the poet had in mind to establish their images. Meanwhile, their images in the original poem have presented the readers with absolute freedom to imagine: one, two or more? The lack of markers in number in Chinese leads to narrowing down the readers' imagination in the translated version, since the number in English has to be clarified in its translated version.

2. Differences in tense markers

In English the tense and aspect of a verb are indicated by the inflections, such as "-ed, -s, and -ing", while in Chinese such tense markers never appear. Thus, a kind of beauty of vagueness resulting from not confining to one particular time or space is created. For example:

Example 3:

ST:

去国离乡二十年,于今衣锦返家园。
蜂采百花成蜜后,为谁辛苦为谁甜?

(《红楼梦》第一百零一回)

TT1:

The one who for a score of years left home
Now in fine raiment will return again.
The honey culled from blossoms by the bee
Is seized by others — all its toil is vain.

(*Yang's translation*)

TT2:

When twenty years away from home have passed,
In silks the wanderer returns at last.
The bee culls nectar from a hundred flowers;
Honey for some, but for himself a thankless task

(*Hawkes' translation*)

In the above versions, the words "left, will turn, culled, have passed, culls..." clearly mark the change of time, although the two translators used different kinds of tense, leaving no vagueness.

3. Differences in personal pronouns

Personal pronouns in English have two sets of case forms: subjective and objective, such as I / me, we / us,... Possessive pronouns play a more vital role in English than that in Chinese. Compared with that in English, the syntactic function of subjects is much weaker in Chinese poetical language in which subjects are frequently omitted. As a result poets do not impose too much their own personalities and sentiments on the scene, for the omitted subjects can be randomly identified with anyone, whether the readers or some imaginary persons. But the omitted subjects must be clarified in English poems when they are translated them into English. For example:

Example 4:

ST:

桃李春风结子完，到头谁似一盆兰。
如冰水好空相妒，枉与他人作笑谈。

（《红楼梦》第五回）

T1:

Peach and plum in spring winds finish seeding,
Who can bloom like the orchid at last?
Pure as ice and water she arouses envy,
Vain the groundless taunts that are cast.

(*Yang's translation*)

T2:

The plum-tree bore her fruit after the rest,
Yet, when all's done, her Orchid was the best.
Against your ice-pure nature all in vain
The tongues of envy wagged; you felt no pain.

(*Hawkes' translation*)

No definite subjects can be found in the original poem, but in Yang's version, he used "she" once, and in Hawkes', he used "her, your, and you", which shows that Hawkes as a native speaker of English uses subjects more frequently than Yang

Xianyi. It's evident that the strategies to deal with the omitted subjects will greatly influence the effects of translation and it's challenging for translators to decide in which way to translate.

Omission is not confined to possessive adjectives. Connective particles are usually omitted in Chinese, which makes Chinese poems possible for the assemblage and juxtaposition of images. Here another example is listed:

Example 5:

ST:

唐多令

粉堕百花洲,香残燕子楼。
一团团,逐对成毬。
漂泊亦如人命薄:……

(《红楼梦》第七十回)

TT1:

Tang-To-Ling

Pink petals fall in Hundred Flowers Islet.
By Swallow Tower their fragrance slowly fades;
Catkins following in clusters
Float off like ill-fated maids;...

(*Yang's translation*)

TT2:

Tang-Duo-Ling

The pollen is spent in the Island of Flowers;
From the House of the swallow the perfume has fled.
The bluff-balls dance,
Pursue, embrace,
Their floating lives, as our lives, quickly sped...

(*Hawkes' translation*)

In the original poem, the two places of "百花洲" and "燕子楼" are used without any modifiers, but when translated into English, the article of "the" or "a" is required by English grammar. However, Yang Xianyi did not obey the rule of using articles before the singular form —"百花洲" and "燕子楼" of countable nouns in English in the first two lines. It can be inferred that "he was trying to be more faithful to the source text or it is just produced by his negligence." (秦希仁, 2007: 23) On the contrary, "the" appeared three times in the first three lines in Hawkes', which seems to be more grammatical.

3.1.3 Difficulties caused by cultural differences

A poem is usually set within a socio-cultural environment, which is the source of creation; therefore, poetry is a mirror reflecting the conditions of a nation's culture. Cultural differences do exist everywhere between different nations. As we know, a specific language is the product of the unique culture of a nation, that's to say, each culture has its own peculiarities, which, manifested in language, are displayed through distinctive features in aspects like cultural habits, custom, wording and rhetorical devices and the like, and in most cases, they are partially untranslatable. When language is used in communication, it is bound up with culture in multiple and complex ways. Raffel concluded "Not two languages having the same literary history, it is impossible to re-create the literary forms of one culture in the language and literary culture of another. Literary forms (structures), like other linguistic structures, have deep roots in a particular culture and a particular language. Every artist's work is conditioned by the limitations of the medium within which he works, by the cultural background in which he has grown up, and by the demands which his culture makes on him. Hence the literature written in any given language is of course channeled... by the structure of the language... The poet works from the outset with a more or less precise pattern into which words and phonemes must fit in order to qualify as a poem of the particular variety he wishes to write... Poems are thus specific to language in a way in which prose literature is not." (Raffel, 1988: 17-18) Although it is hard to define culture, It's widely agreed that culture is described as comprising history, geography, customs, tradition, lifestyle, literature and art, behavioral norms, thinking modes, and values. The following illustrates the influence of culture on the translation of imagery.

Example 6:

ST:

桃花行

桃花帘外东风软，桃花帘内晨妆懒。
帘外桃花帘内人，人与桃花隔不远。……

(《红楼梦》第七十回)

TT1:

Peach-Blossom

Outside the blind, peach-blossom, a soft spring breeze;
Within, a girl is languidly dressing her hair.
Outside, the peach-blossom; within the girl
Not far apart the blossom and maid so fair...

(Yang's translation)

TT2:

The Flower of the Peach

Peach pink the tender flowers outside the window blow;
Peach pink on sleepy face the morning colours glow.
Tree-flowers outside the room and lady-flower inside:
Only a few short steps the flowery forms divid...

(*Hawkes' translation*)

In these two lines, the Chinese "桃" as a kind of fruit "peach" appears four times, but in Chinese poetry, "桃" and "逃" sound the same, "桃" often makes the readers think of

"逃" ("escaping and reclusion"). Therefore the above poem implies Lin Daiyu's loneliness and reclusion, staying in her chamber. Although the poem was written in the bloomy spring, it was filled with a mourning atmosphere. Yet when translating, the translators have no choice but to employ the semantic translation into "peach", losing its original sound as well as its original cultural implication. As a result, when reading its translated version, the western readers have trouble fully understanding its implied meaning of "escaping and reclusion".

Similarly, culture is regional, and the local culture is inevitably reflected by its special geographical environment and climate features. "东风" in the above poem loses its implied meaning in the translated version due to the differences of geographical location. England is an island, situated in the Western Hemisphere with a marine climate. Such phrases as "spend money like water", "make water", and "all at sea" are characterized by its geographical features. On the contrary, China is located in Asia. Therefore, east wind in China stands for "spring and warmth just as Lin Daiyu sings above, "桃花帘外东风软", while east wind in England is cold and unpleasant. The works of *Ode to the West Wind* written by P. B. Shelley to eulogize the season of spring, quoted in *David Copperfield* by Charles Dickens "How many winter days have I seen him, standing blue nosed in the snow and east wind?" is a convincing one to show the difference. The transition from Chinese to

English culture is made tricky because all the images mentioned are unfamiliar to an English reader.

3.2 Reasons for application of the approach of empathy in poetry translation

3.2.1 Theoretical foundations of the approach of empathy in translation

We can draw inspiration from Ingram's understanding of empathy while mentioning the relationship between translation and empathy. Ingram (Ingram, 2001) considers empathy as a kind of "transference". We may find that "empathy" as "transference" is closely related to "translate". Though in modern English they have different meanings and belong to different categories, they are derived from the same root "transferre" according to the etymology. (quoted in潘卫民、钱妮娜, 2006: 51. The translation is mine.)

It seems that translation is a variant of one language at first glance, but if carefully considered, it's definitely hard to deal with. Literary translation is different from non-literary translation. Firstly, literary works are written in literary language that is sentimental, which is intended to express artistic emotion. Secondly, the method of literary translation is artistic and creative. Therefore, literary translation calls for not only the transference of linguistic units, but also the reproduction of the artistic images and styles of the original. Only readers actively imagine, contemplate, resonate and empathize can the beauty of the original be kept and even the non-existent beauty in the original be created.

Besides, the original text, especially when it is a literary work, always includes cultural elements such as sentiments, beliefs, values and attitudes, etc., which can easily lead to linguistic differences, meaning vacancies and misunderstanding. According to the concept of idealization, the absolute equivalence between the ST and the TT can hardly be achieved in intercultural translation regardless of whatever standpoints we take — from the translation of translators or from the acceptance of readers. It's necessary for a translator to actively imagine, appreciate and supplement on the basis of his own understanding, aesthetic and life experience to understand the true feelings and intentions of the author. The sentiment mentioned here refers to a cultural phenomenon. The cultural sentiments contain emotions, attitude, moods, mentalities, beliefs, etc. It is necessary to study the sentimental transference in intercultural translation to make the readers of the TT enjoy the same sentiments. In this sense, poetry translation can be considered as an aesthetic creation and empathy seems necessary for the translator to decode the "cultural symbols" in order to maintain the essence of literary works. Only in this way can the aesthetic values of the original be reproduced.

In Chinese translation field, the issue on sentiments was noticed some time ago. As we know, different translators have different understanding about the “spirit” of works, sometimes this sort of “spirit” is hardly grasped and even more difficult putting into concrete words, particularly in poem, because its spirit is not a substantial object of translation like words or phrases, but a transcendence of the character and words such as images and sentiments, so empathy is particularly needed to convey the unspeakable “spirit” of a poem. For example, the well-respected translator Weng Xianliang once talked about poetry translation and said, “Poetry comes from sentiments and depends on sentiments. As an agent between the poet and its foreign readers, the translator must understand and foster the poet’s sentiments as an actor enters into the spirit of a character. Only in this way can he express similar sentiments in another language.” (翁显良, 1987: 278. The translation is mine.) The process of “fostering the poet’s sentiments” is actually the performance of empathy by the translator to completely reproduce the original artistic images and styles so as to enable readers of the TT to get the same enlightenment, move and aesthetic feeling as the readers of the ST.

1. Feasibility of the approach of empathy

Kant once pointed out that "the necessary condition to appraise judgments is the concept of sensus communis which refers to a necessary psychological law that the joy and loftiness one feels convey to another." (林同华, 1987: 105-106. The translation is mine.) It means that artistic images created by the poet are perceptible. For example, "慈母手中线，游子身上衣" has come down from time immemorial, and still enjoys great popularity. Psychologists after Kant found in their researches that people have the psychological experiences which are based on the direct similarity between the outer things and people's minds, and this psychological law is called Aesthetic Similitude Law. For example, we always associate autumn with solitude; therefore, when the images such as "明岁秋风知再会，暂时分手莫相思"（贾探春《残菊》）；"秋花惨淡秋草黄，耿耿秋灯秋夜长"（林黛玉《代离别·秋窗风雨夕》appear in our mind，we tend to associate them with those things like misery, desolation and apprehend the implications of the poems as if we were on the scene.

Chinese-English poetry has significant differences not only in form but also in ideological contents. In addition, though each national culture seems complicated, the unity is clearly visible behind the variety. Because man has a common ancestor, the more remote people trace back to the history, the less difference they find between different nations. Through the medium of empathy, building a bridge for communication between different language modes, communicative modes and cultural modes is not only necessary but also feasible.

Human thoughts have the characteristics of surpassing time and space, which determines the feasibility and necessity of empathy as well. There coexist a lot of nationalities in the word, and each nationality shares sameness or similarity in the way of thinking. Though poets might live thousands of years ago，the scenery in the poems may exist far away, we can still use image，association and imagination to reach poets' aesthetic feelings and creations. Sentiments including anger, joy, sadness, happiness, and wills, feelings and desires, are complex and cannot be expressed thoroughly in words. Therefore, empathy becomes a necessity in translation. "The concept of commonness of feelings, the Aesthetic Similitude Law and the characteristics of surpassing time and space of thoughts provide bases for aesthetics，psychology and thinking science for the feasibility and necessity of empathetic approach." (卓振英, 2001: 53) Translators are able to exert their imaginations and imitate poets' specific aesthetic models to reproduce, perceive and appreciate poetic images. The life of works can last in time and space through the translator's empathy. A translator is free to imagine travelling through space-time, so as to reappear, reconstruct and appreciate the cultural connotation of the ST. For instance, *Lisao* is one of the works written before 300 B.C by Qu Yuan. When translating it, the translator is supposed to transcend two thousand and three hundred years and the two far-distant continents, have a good knowledge of the social, political conflicts, and then be familiar with Chinese national culture, psychology and traditional aesthetic values at that time. Only by empathizing prudently and repeatedly can he experience and comprehend the quiet atmosphere and magnificent momentum.

2. Scientific nature of the approach of empathy

Wang Guowei (王国维) divided the artistic realm of poetry into "the realm I'm in" and "the realm I'm not in" in his book *Human words and language* (*Renjian Cihua*, 《人间词话》). The former means that "perceiving things through the self, so things are coated with my color". In this realm, "my" sentiments are strong and expressive. The latter refers to "perceiving things through things, so the lines between the things and the self are hard to identify." In this realm, the poet's sentiments pervade in the objective scenery and seem to be concealed and blurred, but as a matter of fact the meaning (意) and the scene (境) are mixed with each other, and things and the self become a unity. Whether "perceiving things through the self" or "perceiving things through things", they will both be involved in the transference of sentiments. It can be seen that empathy is one of the laws in the creation of Chinese poems. It corresponds to this law to regard empathy as a method of examining in Chinese-English poetry translation, which is a kind of imitation or regression to the origin.

"Aesthetics of Acceptance reveals that an aesthetic process is an active re-creative one: on the one hand it is the externalization of the aesthetic ability of the subject; on the other hand it is the spiritualization of the aesthetic characteristics of the object. This kind of double-oriented construction also conforms to the reading appreciation of poetry. Readers are stimulated by the poem, produce aesthetic reaction, perception and absorption, form poetic images in their mind, make their aesthetic perspectives and their aesthetic judgments." (卓振英, 2001: 54. The translation is mine.) For example, after we change the objective existence of Li Shangyin's（李商隐）"春蚕到死丝方尽,蜡炬成灰泪始干" into the images in the subject's mind, we will project the personality of "selfless dedication" into "Laju" (candle) and "Chuncan" (spring silkworm), and the candle and the spring silkworm seem to have the characteristics of a group that make us feel their sublimity. It shows that the poetic appreciation process includes the empathetic process. That translators must experience this process is beyond question.

The process of poetry translation is the process of "changing objective existence into subjective existence, then into a new psychological law that exits objectively." (童庆炳, 1993: 346. The translation is mine.) Poetry translation is a kind of aesthetic recreation, with imagination melting into it definitely. Imagination means the process of rational image thinking to form new images after original images processed on the basis of association. "Translators may innerly imitate the author's sentiments, which are instilled into their imaginary images, and then materialize the fruit of aesthetic creation using the target language, or they may endow the poetic works and the original images with their national, individual and contemporary aesthetic appreciation, make their special explanations, and create more vivid and voluminous artistic images and broader ideorealm." (卓振英, 2001: 54. The translation is mine.) This long-time accumulation of endowment and interpretation is inherited by descendants and becomes filled with artistic vitality. Empathy is involved in both of these two processes. The processing of the original images and the creation of new images are both processes of empathizing, because the so-called images are harmonious integration of the mutually co-existing minds and objects, neither of which is dispensable. This kind of empathizing means it "invites" the poet to take part in the interpretation of the poetic works. Translators can only translate poems with the closet resemblance of both forms and the spiritual charm by enabling themselves enter the role, just as an actor can act perfectly only when he enters into the spirit of a character.

It conforms to the rule of aesthetics of literature and art, aesthetic psychology and thinking science to utilize the approach of empathy in poetry translation, which can be assured through the examination of poetic creation, appreciation and translation.

3. Significance of the approach of empathy

Correct understanding of words and verses relies on the complete grasp of the total concept of the whole poem. In order to grasp the total concept of the poem, translators have to make a profound and meticulous study on the poet and the poem so that they have a pretty good idea of the thought, style, creative background of the poet, the technique of expression, images, artistic conception, connotation, phonology, rhythm, category and form of the poem. This is the so-called Overall Survey. (卓振英, 1997: 44) According to the concept of Overall Survey, it is of great significance to hold the whole imagery of the poem using empathy as a method for Overall Survey to reflect on the poet and his works.

The language user is an important factor of ascertaining the meaning of linguistic signs. Translators can achieve the purpose of emotional communication among aesthetic subjects by way of inspiring their aesthetic perception and aesthetic awareness, and transferring the self into the other by projecting the poet's thoughts and sentiments, which can shorten the psychological distance between the self and the poet. And then the poet's life outlook, world outlook and aesthetic attitude will be thoroughly perceived and interpreted, which is very important to understand the poem correctly. After aesthetic perception, aesthetic sentiments, wills and other information about the poet come into the translators' minds, they will automatically fuse into, connect with each other and activate the translators' aesthetic psychological structure, reorganize and consolidate this structure.

"A relationship of aesthetic empathy is also formed between translators and poetic images, which embodies the emotional exchange of aesthetic activities." (卓振英, 2001: 54. The translation is mine.) This kind of empathy has two meanings. "First, it contributes to the perception and understanding of the connotation of the artistic conception of poems and holding the imagery of them. A translator integrates the poet's sentiments with his own aesthetic experience, visualizes the scenery, and then compares the aesthetic conceptions. Thus the creative images are sure to be perfect, not deficient; and the whole imagery in his mind will be an all-round and multi-dimensional embodiment after the images are fused with each other. Second, it can help produce the target language that accurately materializes poetic images of poems. In poetry translation, images or imagery can act as the media of the mutual transition of the source language and the target language. The psychological process of translation shows this." (卓振英, 2001: 54. The translation is mine.)

3.2.2 Practical foundations of the approach of empathy in translation

It concerns the success of the translation whether the approach of empathy is used in poetry translation or not. From the perspective of Information Theory, translation can be regarded as a process that the information conveyed in one language is expressed in another language. The information includes meaning, ideological content, emotion, style and figure of speech, etc. In the transformation process of information, the involvement of sentiment in translation is crucial to the success of translation. Various instances can be used to prove that it is possible to apply the approach of empathy practically. Here is one:

Example 7:

ST:

鹊桥仙

纤云弄巧，飞星传恨，银汉迢迢暗度。金风玉露一相逢，便胜却人间无数。

柔情似水，佳期如梦，忍顾鹊桥归路。两情若是久长时，又岂在朝朝暮暮。

TT:

Clouds float like works of art,

Stars shoot with grief at heart.

Across the Milky Way the Cowherd meets the Maid.

When Autumn's Golden Wind embraces Dew of Jade,

All the love scenes on earth, however many, fade.

Their tender love flows like a stream;
Their happy date seems but a dream.
How can they bear a separate homeward way?
If love between both sides can last for aye,
Why need thy stay together night and day?

(许渊冲, 2007: 168-169)

This poem expresses the poet's lofty ideals and serious attitude to love, which is intended to sing the praises of the pure love between the Cowherd and the Maid who were separated on the banks and could only feel their tears, and were allowed to meet once a year on the seventh evening of the seventh lunar month. The poet thinks that though the two celestial lovers could only see each other once a year, their gathering is more valuable and happier than any other one on earth. A parenthesis "however many" employed in the translation is to demonstrate countless love scenes on earth and at the same time "fade" to show the author's preference that all these scenes seem inferior compared with that between the Cowherd and the Maid. Besides, the two rhetorical questions "How can they bear a separate homeward way? If love between both sides can last for aye, why need thy stay together night and day?" lay stress on the two lovers' firm beliefs in pure love and their heartbreaking state when confronted with tearing apart from each other, which is appropriate both in the ideological content and linguistic form. From these we can see the translator projected his own feelings into the translation and the version was fully empathized with the poet, in this way, the translator can comprehensively apprehend the author's intention and preference towards love, then render them accurately by rhetorical devices in the target language. In other words, he imitated the poet's aesthetic sentiments, aesthetic perception and aesthetic will inside, experienced the aesthetic process, thus quite successfully empathized with the poet of the original poem.

3.3 Empathetic obstacles in translation

Empathetic obstacles are a complicated psychological issue that the translator will inevitably face in the process of translation, namely, temporal and spatial obstacle, cultural obstacle, psychological obstacle and linguistic obstacle. (刘宓庆, 2005: 226-235)

Bilingual transference is an advanced linguistic activity which must deal with temporal and spatial difference. The source language may be hardly recognized or understood exactly by contemporaries as a result of the development of society and culture, and involution of history. For example, when a translator is translating *Hongloumeng*, he has to transcend more than two hundred years to learn about its social background and aesthetic value of that time. The first major obstacle the time-space difference causes is the correct understanding of the original meaning, which deals with the semantic ambiguity, rhythmic accuracy and a great diversity of aesthetic values. For example, refrains (复叠句) are rich in the Bible, which is a kind of beauty in form that has changed a lot, for they are not utilized in large quantities in contemporary poems except in folk songs and folk rhymes. According to Gu Zhengyang (顾正阳), the obstacles in understanding the original caused by temporal and spatial difference can be overcome as the translator always "choose the one that has the most aesthetic value." (quoted in 韩雨苇,2010: 15)

The obstacle of cultural difference is common in empathy, too. And it is the translator's responsibility to decode the "cultural symbols" in the source language so as to understand the true feelings and intentions of the author. Such cultural symbols with profound connotations are common in literary works, which has been discussed in Chapter 3.1.3.

Aesthetic empathy is usually realized on the basis of the subject's aesthetic experience. The Austrian psychologist Karl Gross (1861—?) and Englishman Veron Lee (1856—1935) put forward the theory of inner mimesis thinking that the successful achievement of aesthetic competence involves a mimetic process motivated by the aesthetic perception. For example, when we are watching a moving drama with the performance understood tacitly, our psychology is changed "from self to object" (the actor's performance). The end of "psychological changing process" marks the end of mimetic process, which satisfies our aesthetics. But the inner mimesis usually should be based on the subject's aesthetic and life experience, without which, it will be very hard for him to go into the mimetic process to fully understand the original.

"The linguistic obstacle in empathy has two implications. One is the linguistic obstacle in a general sense, which has to do with the translator's linguistic competence." (刘宓庆, 2005: 233. The translation is mine.) It's not a serious matter to overcome this kind of obstacle. That's to say, the translator is assumed to be at least bilingual because "understanding and appreciation of the source text are fundamental to any attempts at translating." (Nida, 2001a: 108) "The other refers to the designed obstacle by the translator involved in the original language, which has little to do with the translator's linguistic competence." (刘宓庆, 2005: 233. The translation is mine.)

From the analysis of the above examples, the conclusion can be drawn that the approach of empathy is not only a principle in poetry translation, but also an indispensible method to attain a successful rendition. The process of performing empathy involves the translator's active participation in overcoming empathetic obstacles, and the role of subjectivity of language and translator in empathy will be further discussed in Chapter Seven. More examples and similar analyses will be introduced in the next chapters, in which a comparison between the two English translations of poetry in *Hongloumeng* from the perspective of empathy will be discussed.

Chapter Four
Comparison of Aesthetic Empathy in Poetry Translation in *Hongloumeng*

4.1 *Hongloumeng* and its two translated versions

4.1.1 Poetry in *Hongloumeng*

“中国说部,登峰造极者,无若石头记,叙人间富贵,盛人情盛衰,用笔缜密,著色繁丽,制精严,观止矣”(林纾)(Chinese fiction reaches its culmination in *the Dream of the Red Chamber*, so far as it narrates the changes of fortune and the vicissitudes of life, in a refined, meticulous style, with rich, varied colourings and a carefully worked-out overall plan, it is perfection itself.) As is well known, *Hongloumeng*, together with *San Guo Yan Yi (The Three Kingdoms)*, *Shui Hu Zhuan (Outlaws of Marsh)*, and *Xi You Ji (The Journey to the West)*, is honored as one of the four masterpieces of fiction in China's Ming and Qing Period.

The majority of the researchers believe that the immortal novel of *Hongloumeng* was written by Cao Xueqin (1715—1763) and Gao E (1740—1815). It took Cao Xueqin over a period of two decades to work on the version of his novel originally called

Shitouji (The Story of the Stone), but he left the work unfinished. This eighty-chapter version, which was accompanied by a commentary by Red Inkstone had been circulated in manuscript among friends when the author was still alive. It was not until 1792 that a complete 120-chapter edition carefully edited and supplemented by Cao E and printed by Cheng Weiyuan became available under the title of *Hongloumeng*.

The writer of Cao Xueqin took the tragically unfulfilled love of Jai Baoyu, the hero, for a temperamental and delicate girl named Lin Daiyu as its main thread, centering on which, he described the prosperity and decline of an aristocratic household against a broad social background. He exposed all kinds of tricks, treacheries, and irrationality of the social morality, legality and ideology of the age. With deep sympathy and affection, he succeeded in depicting the individuality and personality of the heroes and heroines. They are in their tragical rebellion against their lots, striving for freedom in the hope of a better life against chains of the traditional ethical code, but all in vain. It penetratingly revealed the luxury, corruption and evil of the feudal society, exposed ruthless exploitation of the laboring people by the upper-class and mirrored the doomed ending of the decayed feudal society. By exposing the darkness in social life, he sang the elegy over the fate of the whole social mansion which was on the verge of total collapse. In his works, Cao Xueqin also showed his own rebellion spirit against the old-aged creed "literature for the sake of conveying the Confucian Tao (truth)" and made a sweeping condemnation on the Neo-Confucianist preaching "extinguishing the human desire." The novelist created a series of characters to pay homage to human nature and human sentiments.

Cao Xueqin is a poet as well as a novelist, whose linguistic and artistic achievements represent the climax of classical Chinese literature. Through the poems which are supposed to be written by the teenage heroes and heroines of the novel, we can find out their own personality and views on the contemporary society. Though most of the poems are written by the female characters, they still serve to demonstrate Cao Xueqin's versatility in his writing style. In addition, the poems are quite different from those in other novels of his time which are doggerels of the same type. There are more than two hundred and fifty poems in *Hongloumeng*, covering various genres, such as lyric meters (*ci*), poems (*shi*), dramatic lyrics (*qu*), elegy (*lei*), riddles (*mi*) and so on. No other works can compare with it in its amazingly rich and broad cultural connotation. And none can surpass it in its successful use of poems, lyric meters, lyrics and expositions and other forms to reflect the personalities and fates of the major characters, which are not only of high aesthetic value, but help to establish typical personalities and develop the plot of the story. The repertoire of those verses is like a garden in full blossom, where诗、词、曲、赋 and other forms are a variety of flowers, contributing their charm and composing a wonderful picturesque view. Such colorful and varied poetical forms have seldom been found in any other classical Chinese novels ever since; thus the richness and profoundness of Chinese culture is presented before the readers' eyes. The poems in *Hongloumeng* are not only up to the frame of embodying diversiform style but also merge into the narration as an organic component, and fulfill the author's overall consideration, and they are an inseparable part of the whole, embody the author's painstaking arrangement and intentions. They function mainly in three aspects.

Firstly, when readers are reading the poems in *Hongloumeng*, it's easy to understand the characters' personalities and destiny. In *Hongloumeng*, dozens of major characters are portrayed successfully including men and women, aristocrats and servants. The poems in it have a unique feature; that is, Cao Xueqin prepared different poems for different characters according to their specific personalities. For example, Lin Daiyu is regarded as the most talented maiden, who was an exclusive orphan living under her uncle's roof and in the hopeless love with Baoyu, which fills her poems with despair, sentimentality and lamentation. The lines "一年三百六十天，风刀霜箭严相逼" portray the harsh conditions in her eyes; "一朝春尽红颜老，花落人亡两不知" displays her despair;"两弯似蹙非蹙罥烟眉，一双似喜非喜含情目"reflects her looks of wisdom, beauty and sentiment. Hence, her personalities are not only presented by her words and deeds but also revealed in the poems she composed. What's more, the personalities of the other major characters are revealed in poems concerned as well, such as the characters of modesty and loyalty to the social conventions of Xue Baochai, and the ignorant and indecent character of Xue Pan. At the same time, the poems indicate the fate of the characters. For example, in Chapter Five, the *First Registers of Twelve Beauties in Jingling* and twelve songs named *A Dream of Red Mansions* gives the outline of the fate of the girls in Grand View Garden. "玉带林中挂，金簪雪里埋" indicates the tragic ending of Daiyu and Baochai; "清明涕送江边望，千里东风一梦遥" shows Tanchun's marrying far away and no chance to come back; "可怜绣侯门女，独卧青灯古佛旁" reveals Xichun's ending in a lonely nun life.

Secondly, the poems display the spiritual and cultural life of that time. To be proficient in versification was taken by the well-educated and refined nobilities as a fashion in ancient times especially in the Qing Dynasty, when poets' club was so popular among well-educated nobilities. In *Hongloumeng*, through the description of scenes of poetizing and making-up riddles in such an aristocratic family as the Jias, aspects of spiritual life of the gerentocratic class in the Qing Dynasty have been reflected. The visit of Jia Yuanchun to her parents on the Feast of Lanterns is looked on as an indication of the trips of the Qing emperors to the south. Then the extemporization in "the Grand View Garden" can be considered as the officials extemporizing before emperors.

Thirdly, it satirizes the corruption and moral degeneration of the Qing Dynasty. All in all, the poetry in it highlights the theme of the novel and foreshadows subsequent development of the story.

We Chinese appreciate it with joy and pride. How can the readers in other cultures share this Chinese treasure? Clearly the answer is that we can make it by way of translation.

4.1.2 About the two English versions of *Hongloumeng*

We are proud and delighted that *Hongloumeng* has aroused more and more interest overseas. Up to now, it has been translated into different versions in nearly eighty languages. Just for English readers, there are nearly 10 translations of excerpts or complete edition of the novel, among which the two best-known are *A Dream of Red Mansions* by Yang Xianyi and Gladys Yang and *The Story of the Stone* by David Hawkes and John Minford, and the birth of them fill the blanks of the translation of classical Chinese literature. The works provide precious experiences and insights for the translation of Chinese classics, especially verse translation, and providing new direction or way of thinking in translation. It's worthwhile to study them carefully. Another thing that has to be mentioned is that we have to know about the background of the two translators, which helps us understand the great works, too.

In 1978 and 1979, a complete edition of *A Dream of Red Mansions* with one hundred and twenty chapters was published in three volumes by the Foreign Language Press of China. Yang Xianyi, the chief translator, was born in an intellectual family and deeply bred in the classical Chinese literature. So he cherished great emotions and feelings for the traditional culture. Meanwhile, his wife, Gladys Yang, majoring in Chinese literature in Oxford University, also cast an impressive influence on his works and gave a great help in the process of translation. As we can see, both of them got a thorough understanding of oriental culture and Western culture, so their match is a combination of Chinese and English cultures.

The Story of the Stone marked the start of its complete translation in the west. Penguin Books Ltd of England published its first 26 chapters in 1973 and it was not until 1986 that the complete novel got its last chapter into print. The whole version was composed of five volumes and the last two volumes (the translation of Gao E's 40 chapters) were finished by Hawkes' son-in-law, John Minford. David Hawkes was a student of Arthur Waley, a reputable British sinologist. He studied Chinese at Oxford University from 1945 to 1948 and was a research student at Peking University from 1948 to 1951, before he tried *Hongloumen*g, he had translated a large amount of works by many famous Chinese ancient poets like Qu Yuan and Du Fu, etc.

"Despite different styles presented in these two versions, both of them achieved the goals by their translators. The version by David Hawkes is famous for its elegance, while Yang Xianyi and Gladys Yang's is remarkable for accuracy... If reading them together, those who are unable to read the original will acquire the real and complete picture about this novel as they do read." (周钰良, 1994: 350)

At the same time, the renowned redologist Wu Shichang once commented that he has read the translation sentence by sentence and word by word in contrast to the Zhijing (Gengcheng) manuscript, and *A Dream of Red Mansions* was the most complete and precise among the present English translations.

In the following parts, a detailed comparison will be made to study the two versions from the perspective of aesthetic empathy, cultural empathy and pragmatic empathy with special regard to the translation of poetry in *Hongloumeng*.

4.2 Comparison of aesthetic empathy

Poems originate from feelings and emotions. As is explained in the previous chapters, poems are multi-faceted and condensed expressions in certain forms that carry style, images, and music as reflections of the innermost emotion and thought of a poet, including sorrows, pains, frustration, distress, depression, peacefulness, contentedness, happiness, joy, smile, laughter, and the like. They are yells or laughs from the poet's innermost heart, songs chanted from the soul, pictures drawn from imagination, and utterances given in language with words and lines in shapes and styles.

In sum, poetry translation is to enable TL readers to feel the same aesthetic and emotional values as the SL readers do. Then how to transfer the original so that the TL readers can get similar aesthetic experiences as the SL readers do in meaning, sound and from? To be specific, Professor Xu Yuanchong raised the principle of "three beauties" for poetry translation, which requires translators to consider from three aspects when translating poems, namely, beauties in sense, sound and form. (许渊冲, 1984: 52-61. The translation is mine.) "In order to translate Chinese poems into international treasure, it is necessary to try to convey their beauty in sense, sound and form in the original poems." (许渊冲, 2003: 42. The translation is mine.) The "three aesthetic aspects" are actually united as an organic whole in a poem, so that the translator should take pains to convey the "three aesthetic aspects" simultaneously as far possible. It is important to transfer the unique aesthetics in Chinese poems in poetry translation, because the aesthetic transference of sense, sound and form in the original poem will be greatly beneficial for sentimental transference to achieve good poetry translation.

4.2.1 Aesthetic empathy in terms of sense

Someone once compared the form and sound of the regulated verse to the bone and flesh of a body and the sense to the soul of it (常谢枫, 1995). Sense, a term in Chinese classical aesthetics, refers to the writer's subjective and its artistic expression in his or her works; it is his or her internal aesthetic experience, cognition, and interests in the real environment; it forms the score of artistic creation in China. Though stirred by the real world, it is commonly considered to occur in the mental world. (刘玉梅, 2004: 38) The simplest as well as the broadest definition of sense, according to the *Longman Dictionary* (1995), is meaning — that which you intend to understand by something spoken or written, or by something expressed in other way, such as sighs. Generally speaking, the realization of sense is achieved by the lexical, semantic and pragmatic levels of language combined. Xu Yuanchong states that "in the translation of Tang Poems, the most important task for a translator to do is to reproduce the beauty in sense." (Xu Yuanchong, 1992: 113) And Nida defines translation as "the reproduction in a receptor language of the closest natural equivalent to the source language message, first in terms of meaning, and secondly in terms of style." (Nida and Taber, 1982: 208) It is quite reasonable that meaning is of vital importance in all types of messages. Translation, as a means of communication, helps readers get the same message of the original text. To achieve this, a translator should have a thorough comprehension of the original content and spirit before he starts his work. Professor Xu points out that "'beautiful sense' does not refer to the surface meaning but the deep meaning — image and artistic conception." (Xu Yuanchong, 1992: 122) The translation should be first faithful to the content and at the same time should pay enough attention to the reproduction of images, which will involve the matter of expression —style. Appreciation of poetry is to explore its deep implication by reading the surface of it. "Poetry exists beyond its language (诗在言外)," which is what people call "poetic value (诗意)". As for the Chinese poetry, the most refined art, the sense of it includes a deeper layer of definition. That is the artistic conception (意境, Yijing), or the style, or the atmosphere which is created by the poet and the two basic forming elements in sense are the image that the poet chooses and the feeling that the poet expresses. (陈威, 2008: 23) Angus C. Graham (1988) asserts that the translation of image is fundamental since it is the essence of poetry. He says that "the element in poetry which travels best is of course concrete imagery" and "the essence of poetry is the image." (quoted in 黄河清, 2008: 3) And Xu Yuanchong in his principle of "three-aspect beauty", puts the beauty in sense in the first place, which is mainly conveyed through images. As the basic unit for the construction of artistic conception, image is the primary concern for classical Chinese poetry in the aesthetic sense.

Yi is the subjective thoughts and feeling; Jing is the objective life and scenes. The artistic conception is composed of two elements: feeling and image. The inner feeling and the outside image mix together and affect each other, as feelings emerge with scenes or images, and scenes relive with feelings. Artistic conception is an important category in Chinese aesthetic thoughts, embodying artistic beauty, which, usually considered as one of the measuring standards in artistic creation, appreciation and criticism, is the soul of classical poems, too. So it is important to express well the artistic conception in literary translation, especially in poetry translation. The following examples will illustrate how the two translators handle the two aspects of artistic conception.

1. The handling of image

As the most important material carrier of the sense, image is central to all poetry. "G. E. Lessing (1729—1781) said that imagery is the sensuous impression produced in poetry *(Laoccoon)*. Ezra Pound (1885—1973) defined imagery as 'an intellectual and emotional complex'." (quoted in 朱徽, 1996: 20) Robert Frost also comments that "image and after-imagery are about all there is to poetry." (quoted in Parini, 1987: 27) Image combined with the poet's feelings to produce a picturesque artistic conception functions importantly in such aspects as expressing effectively the feeling of the poet, forming the unique style of the poet, making the abstract concept concrete and vivid, and increasing the artistic influence of the poetry. To a certain extent, the successful rendering of the original images means the success of the translation of sense.

Many poems in *Hongloumeng* are rich in images to be in accordance with the design of the story and the characters' personalities, which are well embodied between described objective view and expressional thought and sentiment. They create the artistic conception to convey the profound sentiments of the composers. Because image constitutes the most vivid and beautiful part of condensed and compact classical Chinese poetry, the treatment of image during the process of translating classical Chinese poetry into English involves much perplexity. Now take *the Song of Flower-Burial* ("葬花吟") as an example.

Example 8:

ST:

葬花吟

花谢花飞花满天，红消香断有谁怜？
游丝软系飘春榭，落絮轻沾扑绣帘。
闺中女儿惜春暮，愁绪满怀无释处；
手把花锄出绣帘，忍踏落花来复去。
柳丝榆荚自芳菲，不管桃飘与李飞；
桃李明年能再发，明年闺中知有谁？

三月香巢已垒成，梁间燕子太无情。
明年花发虽可啄，却不道人去梁空巢也倾。
一年三百六十日，风刀霜剑严相逼；
明媚鲜妍能几时，一朝漂泊难寻觅。
花开易见落难寻，阶前愁煞葬花人；
独倚花锄泪暗洒，洒上空枝见血痕。
杜鹃无语正黄昏，荷锄归去掩重门；
青灯照壁人初睡，冷雨敲窗被未温。
怪奴底事倍伤神？半为怜春半恼春：
怜春忽至恼忽去，至又无言去不闻。
昨宵庭外悲歌发，知是花魂与鸟魂？
花魂鸟魂总难留，鸟自无言花自羞；
愿奴胁下生双翼，随花飞到天尽头。
天尽头，何处有香丘？
未若锦囊收艳骨，一抔净土掩风流；
质本洁来还洁去，强于污淖陷渠沟。
尔今死去侬收葬，未卜侬身何日丧？
侬今葬花人笑痴，他年葬侬知是谁？
试看春残花渐落，便是红颜老死时；
一朝春尽红颜老，花落人亡两不知！

（《红楼梦》第二十七回）

TT1:

As blossoms fade and fly across the sky,
Who pities the faded red, the scent that has been?
Softly the gossamer floats over spring pavilions,

Gently the willow fluff wafts to the embroidered screen.
A girl in her chamber mourns the passing of spring,
No relief from anxiety her poor heart knows;
Hoe in hand she steps through her portal,
Loath to tread on the blossom as she comes and goes.
Willows and elms, fresh and verdant,
Care not if peach and plum blossom drift away;
Next year the peach and plum blossom will bloom again,
But her chamber may stand empty on that day.
By the third month the scented nests are built,
But the swallows on the beam are heartless all;
Next year, though once again you may peck the buds,
From the beam of an empty room your nest will fall.
Each year for three hundred and sixty days
The cutting wind and biting frost contend.
How long can beauty flower fresh and fair?
In a single day wind can whirl it to its end.
Fallen, the brightest blooms are hard to find;
With aching heart their grave-digger comes now
Alone, her hoe in hand, her secret tears
Falling like drops of blood on each bare bough.
Dusk falls and the cuckoo is silent;
Her hoe brought back, the lodge is locked and still;
A green lamp lights the wall as sleep enfolds her,
Cold rain pelts the casement and her quilt is chill.

What causes my two-fold anguish?
Love for spring and resentment of spring;
For suddenly it comes and suddenly goes,
Its arrival unheralded, noiseless its departing.
Last night from the courtyard floated a sad song--
Was it the soul of blossom, the soul of birds,
Hard to detain, the soul of blossom or birds?
For blossoms have no assurance, birds no words.
I long to take wing and fly
With the flowers to earth's uttermost bound;
And yet at earth's uttermost bound
Where can a fragrant burial mound be found?
Better shroud the fair petals in silk
With clean earth for their outer attire;
For pure you came and pure shall you go,
Not sinking into some foul ditch or mire.
Now you are dead I come to bury you;
None has divined the day when I shall die;
Men laugh at my folly in burying fallen flowers,
But who will bury me when dead I lie?
See, when spring draws to a close and flowers fall,
This is the season when beauty must ebb and fade;
The day that spring takes wing and beauty fades
Who will care for the fallen blossom or dead maid?

(Yang's translation)

TT2:

The blossoms fade and falling fill the air,
Of fragrance and bright hues bereft and bare.
Floss drifts and flutters round the Maiden's bower,
Or softly strikes against her curtained door.
The Maid, grieved by these signs of spring's decease,
Seeking some means her sorrow to express,
Has rake in hand into the garden gone,.
Before the fallen flowers are trampled on.
Elm-pods and willow-floss are fragrant too;
Why care, Maid, where the fallen flowers blew?
Next year, when peach and plum-tree bloom again,
Which of your sweet companions will remain?
This spring the heartless swallow built his nest
Beneath the eaves of mud with flowers compressed.
Next year the flowers will blossom as before,
But swallow, nest, and Maid will be no more.
Three hundred and three-score the year's full tale:
From swords of frost and from the slaughtering gale
How can the lovely flowers long stay intact,
Or, once loosed, from their drifting fate draw back?
Blooming so steadfast, fallen so hard to find!
Beside the flowers' grave, with sorrowing mind,
The solitary Maid sheds many a tear,
Which on the boughs as bloody drops appear.

At twilight, when the cuckoo sings no more,
The Maiden with her rake goes in at door
And lays her down between the lamplit walls,
While a chill rain against the window falls.
I know not why my heart's so strangely sad,
Half grieving for the spring and yet half glad:
Glad that it came, grieved it so soon was spent.
So soft it came, so silently it went!
Last night, outside, a mournful sound was heard:
The spirits of the flowers and of the bird.
But neither bird nor flowers would long delay,
Bird lacking speech, and flowers too shy to stay.
And then I wished that I had wings to fly
After the drifting flowers across the sky:
Across the sky to the world's farthest end,
The flowers' last fragrant resting-place to find.
But better their remains in silk to lay
And bury underneath the wholesome clay,
Pure substances the pure earth to enrich,
Than leave to soak and stink in some foul ditch.
Can I, that these flowers' obsequies attend,
Divine how soon or late *my* life will end?
Let others laugh flower-burial to see:
Another year who will be burying me?
As petals drop and spring begins to fail,

The bloom of youth, too, sickens and turns pale.
One day, when spring has gone and youth has fled.
The Maiden and the flowers will both be dead.

(*Hawkes' translation*)

Ancient Chinese regard implicitness as beautiful and ancient Chinese poets are all concerned with presenting the essence of a mood through the description of a certain scene rather than a direct description of such mood. We can see that this poem creates a sort of sorrowful and desolate atmosphere, by using verbs such as谢、消、断、怜、逼、杀、恼、伤、无、悲、陷、死、葬、残、尽、老、亡; some nouns such as 愁绪、血痕、泪、无尽头, etc.; and by clustering a series of images, such as 春榭、落絮、秀帘、柳丝、芳菲、黄昏、青灯、冷雨、香丘、艳骨. "Flower-Burial" occurs in the late spring, a season full of gloomy moods. These images seem isolated, but they are cleverly arranged by the poet to produce a united, harmonious and complete late spring scene, as a result Daiyu's mixed sentiments of self-pity, helplessness, and discontent are naturally created. And the poem is mixed with anger too. "一年三百六十日，风刀霜剑严相逼" is not meant to flowers, but herself; "愿奴胁下生双翼，随花飞到天尽头" expresses her longing for nice life-style, all of which are purposefully designed by Cao Xueqin for Lin Daiyu. It is doubtless that Yang Xianyi and Hawkes must have taken great pains to reproduce this poem.

Generally speaking, in Yang's translation, most of the

images have been translated literally. The corresponding verbs are "fade, fly, float, waft, mourn, whirl, fall, bury etc; the nouns are anxiety, tears, drops of blood, uttermost bound etc; the images are "gossamer, willow fluff, willows and elms, flesh and verdant, dusk, green lamp lights and so on. In the first stanza, the literal translation "blooms fade and fly across the sky" is combined with the use of alliteration (fade and fly) and internal rhyme (fly, sky) opened the scene. Yang used an interrogation and the literal translation of "pities" and "the faded red" to embody the melancholy feeling in spring, the two verbs of "float" and "waft" expressed the drift and helplessness not only of "gossamer and willow fluff", but also of the poet herself as well as the images of春榭、落絮、秀帘. By contrast, Hawkes merely listed the images in his translation, and simplified "游丝落絮" to "Floss", resulting in the loss of beauty of antithesis in Chinese poetry. In the third stanza, Yang's translation of "willows and elms, fresh and verdant, Care not if peach and plum blossom drift away" accurately reproduced the images, and the words of "care not" agreed with the artistic conception of the original. As a result the discontent with inconstancy of human relationships and social snobbery was reproduced successfully. On the contrary, obviously Hawkes was unable to grasp the original intension, and the images were weakened for the sake of simplicity and legibility. Images in the seventh stanza are also intensively distributed, such as "杜鹃", "重门", "青灯" and

"冷雨" that are special in classical Chinese poetry. "the cuckoo is silent" in Yang's translation presented the deserted atmosphere all of a sudden to set off Daiyu's loneliness perfectly, which was better than "the cuckoo sings no more" in Hawkes'. The major image in "青灯照壁" is "青灯" not "壁", "A green lamp lights the wall" in Yang's highlighted not only the action of lighting but also the image of "青灯". But the head in "the lamplit walls" in Hawkes' is "walls", "青" was omitted as well as the artistic conception of loneliness, quietness and cold. In the ninth stanza, Hawkes translated "庭外" into "outside" in order for the acceptability of the translated version, which ruined certain beauty of artistic conception. The word "floated" in Yang's rendered the feeling of drift of "发" in the original. In the eleventh stanza, "shroud" and "attire" were used by Yang as two images to express the deep implication in the original. In the last stanza, the atmosphere of desolation came to a climax with the employment of "一朝春尽红颜老,花落人亡两不知". Hawkes translated "红颜" into "youth" in the method of deepening. Yang utilized the interrogation to better reflect Daiyu's sad life. What's more, the poem has been divided into thirteen stanzas, with end rhyme used in each even line in every stanza, which is conductive to the conveyance of the beauty in sense.

It can be seen that in dealing with the images in poetry translation, both Yang and Hawkes have a lot in common, and reproduce the artistic conception of the original faithfully to a certain degree. In dealing with the details of images, Yang uses the literal translation to faithfully reproduce the artistic conception and the style of the original, while Hawkes uses a relatively free method. Hawkes' whole translation sounds so beautiful and even bleak when it is read aloud. For example, a large number of words expressing ill-omen are used to create the dismal and lonesome atmosphere, such as "grieved, decease, sorrow, heartless, mournful, grave, and dead."

2. The handling of feeling

Feeling plays a very important role in the creation of mood, too. In his book, Xi Yongji points that "in order to expand the scope of appreciation of beauty, writers usually employ the law of the feelings interlink to fully motivate the sense of sight, listening, smell, taste and touch to perceive the system from different angles, thus give readers the feeling that they are there in person in the process of appreciation." (奚永吉, 2001: 287. The translation is mine.)

Example 9:

ST:

春夜即事

霞绡云幄任铺陈,隔巷蟆更听未真。
枕上轻寒窗外雨,眼前春色梦中人。
盈盈烛泪因谁泣,点点花愁为我嗔。

自是小环娇懒惯,拥衾不耐笑言频。

(《红楼梦》第二十三回)

TT1:

Spring Night

The walls flaunt hangings as sunset clouds
To muffle the frogs' croaking in the lane;
The rain outside the window chills my pillow,
This vision of spring seems like the girl of my dreams.
The candle sheds slow tears—for whom?
The blossoms fall as if reproaching me;
My maids are indolent from long indulgence;
Wearied by their laughter and prattle, I snuggle down in my quilt.

(*Yang's translation*)

TT2:

Spring

Behind silk hangings, in warm quilts cocooned,
His ears half doubt the frogs' first muted sound.
Rain at his window strikes, the pillow's cold;
Yet to the sleeper's eyes spring dreams unfold.
Why does the candle shed its waxen tear?
Why on each flower do angry drops appear?
By uncouth din of giggling maids distressed
He burrows deeper in his silken nest.

(*Hawkes' translation*)

The first line"霞绡云幄任铺陈,隔巷蟆更听未真" means "He feels sleepless with the quilt cocooned and the silk hanging, the frogs' croaking in the lane." "Bright as sunset clouds" in Yang's translation has produced visual effect in color, while "Behind silk hangings, in warm quilts cocooned" in Hawkes' fails to reproduce the visual beauty that "霞绡云幄" has, "warm quilt" and "the pillow's cold" in the third line together provides a sharp contrast with the chill implied. A static picture is presented by " 任 铺 陈 " in the original poem. The two prepositions "behind" and "in" in Hawkes' version are better at reproducing the static picture in the original poem than "The walls flaunt" in Yang's. In the second line, "croaking" with the meaning of ill omen and inauspiciousness in English in Yang's doesn't tie in with the romantic and sweet atmosphere in the original poem; on the contrary, "half doubt" and "first muted sound" in Hawkes' precisely expresses the feeling of dim sound implied in "隔巷蛙声". The second and third lines "枕上轻寒窗外雨,眼前春色梦中人。/ 盈盈烛泪因谁泣,点点花愁为我嗔。" depict Baoyu's longing for Daiyu. On the chilly early spring night, the sight strikes a chord in Baoyu's heart, and the image of Daiyu's sentimental weakness and "点点花愁" as her rebuke to him is revealed to readers clearly. It can been concluded that Yang's translation of "The rain outside the window chills my pillow, / This vision of spring seems like the girl of my dreams." from the angle of the first person is interrelated with "The candle sheds slow tears—for whom? / The blossoms fall as if reproaching me;" in the third stanza, at the same time, "for whom?", "As if reproaching me" exactly communicates Baoyu's tenderness and affection. Compared with Yang's, the translation of "Rain at his window strikes, the pillow's cold; / Yet to the sleeper's eyes spring dreams unfold." in Hawkes' version from the angle of the third person is not as good as that from the angle of the first person of Yang's at conveying Baoyu's true feeling. "Why does the candle shed its waxen tear?" in the third line is only a kind of description of the objective scene; the word "angry" in "Why on each flower do angry drops appear?" is inferior to the word "reproaching" in Yang's in terms of the effective meaning of "嗔". In classical Chinese literature, every twinkle and smile as well as displeasure and joy makes a person filled with sense of beauty. So careful comparison of the two versions shows that Yang accurately reproduced the artistic conception of the feeling and setting happily blended and the identity of object and self from the angle of the first person; however, as to the rendering of Mr. Hawkes', the artistic conception embodied in the original poem is turned into a description of objective scenes from the angle of the third person, with the feelings of the personages lost, which is related with the theory of septum (隔) and undivided (不隔) in poetry translation. Zhu Guangqian points out in *Commentary on the Book of Songs* that the difference between septum and undivided is reflected in terms of the relationship of sentiments and images. Sentiments together with images that can be seen and sentiments felt form undivided. On the contrary, the septum occurs when the images are vague and hollow, the sentiments are superficial, neither of which is trying to impress the readers by the profound world (境界). (朱光潜, 1997:47. The translation is mine.) In the original poem, the images of "霞绡云幄", "隔巷蟆", "窗外雨", "盈盈烛泪" and "点点花愁" and the images of "听未真", "眼前春色梦中人", "因谁泣" and "为我嗔" are blended into a unity with the result of the feeling and setting happily blended, all of which lead to the "undivided" of the artistic conception. All in all, Yang's translation of "The rain outside the window chills my pillow, / This vision of spring seems like the girl of my dreams. / The candle sheds slow tears—for whom? / The blossoms fall as if reproaching me" retained the original empathetic method and reproduced the original "undivided" of the artistic conception. In contrast, Hawkes' translation of "Rain at his window strikes, the pillow's cold; / Yet to the sleeper's eyes spring dreams unfold. / Why does the candle shed its waxen tear? / Why on each flower do angry drops appear?" was unable to integrate the characters and things, feeling and setting with one another; as a result, the original "undivided" was turned into "septum".

"Beauty of images" in poetry is the "beauty of artistic conception" rather than the "picturesque beauty" or "musical beauty". "Artistic conception" is a sort of artistic atmosphere as an intertwined product of images, feelings and sentiments blending. So for Xu Yuanchong, the beauty of the artistic conception of the original refers to its deep structure instead of its surface structure, and it should be reproduced on the level of the deep structure, namely, something that comes from, but goes beyond the text, instead of a word-for-word or line-for-line translation of the verbal meaning of the original. That's to say, he emphasizes the reproduction of the source poem' aesthetic effect. It can be perceived that in the handling of original feeling, there is a very important element that influences the expression of the original and the readers' reaction, that is the angle of person that the translator takes.

4.2.2 Aesthetic empathy in terms of sound

Poetry can never go without musical sound as its power flows from the beauty of sound. It is certain that sound is one component contributing to the beauty and charm of poetry. From the angle of ontology, meaning is closely related to sound and is based on phonetic material. Poems were first written for performance, deriving from oral traditions and presenting themselves to the sensuous intuition and apprehension. The pleasure from poetry lies in the articulation of words and independent dance on vocal organs. The musicality implies some kind definiteness, coherence, or shape existing in a poem as an indispensable part in a harmonious whole, which always arouses our pleasure. So prominent is this musical quality of poetry that many scholars have made it the distinguishing term in their definition of poetry. (李晓红, 2007: 40) According to Professor Xu Yuanchong, to convey the beauty in sound is to convey the beauty in rhyme and rhythm in the original. And if it is possible for the translator to adopt English words which sound similar to the original, it will be better. These penetrating views both in China and in the West have demonstrated the significance of musical quality in poetry indition and appreciation. (quoted in 刘玉梅, 2004: 50)

4.2.2.1 Rhythm and rhyme in Poetry

As known to all, rhythm is common for any literary works, both poetic and non-poetic, with the difference in degree of rigidity. The poems in *Hongloumeng* also have strong musical traits whose major element is rhythm. According to the *Longman Dictionary* (1995), rhythm means the regularly repeated pattern of sound. Rhythm exists everywhere, especially in sound, like continuous waves. Music, especially rock music, depends heavily on rhythm for effects the audiences enjoy, and for regulated verses, their aesthetic value much lies in their chanting. Rhythm is also a powerful tool that a poet uses chiefly to construct a mood and to create a response suitable to the sense of him and ideas. When we are reading a line of poem, we can find that a sequence of stressed and unstressed syllables create regular, or nearly regular, rhythm.

The rhythm of Chinese poems is decided by two factors. The first one is the organization of syllables. Chinese is known as a tone language, in which tones are used to distinguish words, i. e. to differentiate meanings. Each Chinese character is represented by one syllable. For the regulated verse, the number of syllables in each line is fixed and these syllables are not isolated from each other. Generally the rhythm of Chinese poem mainly lies in "pause". In reading a poem, people naturally divide a sentence or a verse into several groups. The division of syllables into "pauses" is based on the consideration of both the neatness of the number of the syllables and the completion of the meaning of the phrases. For a pentasyllabic regulated verse, there should be three "pauses" while for a heptasyllabic one there should be four. For example,

中秋对月有怀口占一律

未卜 / 三生 / 愿，
频添 / 一段 / 愁。
闷来 / 时敛 / 额，
行去 / 几回 / 头。
自顾 / 风前 / 影，
谁堪 / 月下 / 俦？
蟾光 / 如有 / 意，

先上 / 玉人 / 楼。

（《红楼梦》第一回）

凝晖钟瑞（匾额）

芳园 / 筑向 / 帝城 / 西，
华日 / 祥云 / 笼罩 / 奇。
高柳 / 喜迁 / 莺出 / 谷，
修篁 / 时待 / 凤来 / 仪。
文风 / 已着 / 宸游 / 夕，
孝道 / 应隆 / 归省 / 时。
睿藻 / 仙才 / 盈彩 / 笔，
自惭 / 何敢 / 再为 / 辞。

（《红楼梦》第十八回）

Besides the organization of syllables, another important factor in the formation of classical Chinese poetry's rhythm is rhyme, which is essential in achieving the unparalleled musicality in poetry. Many people even draw it from the rhythm and rank it as the equal of the rhythm. In Chinese poetry, when rhyme is mentioned, it refers to end rhyme specifically. The repetition of the similar sound recalls earlier words, emphasizes certain points and creates a rehearsaling atmosphere, like the drums in rock, which appear in regular intervals.

For English poems, "regular patterns of stressed and unstressed syllables are called meters." (Gill, 1985: 34) Since English is a stress language, rhythm in poetry is realized through the flowing of stressed and unstressed syllables, which could be quantified by foot and meter. A unit of poetic meter of stressed and unstressed syllables is foot, which is applied with a single line, indicating how many meters are employed in that line. A foot can be composed of two or three syllables, one of which must be stressed. “Foot” has its own significance in poetry translation. The reason is that many translators choose different foot patterns to create various poetic metrics in their translations. Here are five commonly used patterns:

Iambic: an unstressed syllables followed by a stressed one;

Anapaestic: two unstressed syllables followed by a stressed one;

Trochaic: a stressed syllable followed by an unstressed one;

Dactylic: a stressed syllable followed by two unstressed ones;

Spondaix: two successive stressed syllables.

When we analyze the rhythm of an English poem, we should first define its metrical pattern, and then find out how many feet it includes and get its characteristic at last. Meter is the measurement of the number of feet. It differs from one another because of the different number of feet. The number of the stressed syllables equals that of the feet, Following are names for feet: monometer (one foot), diameter (two feet), trimester (three feet), tetrameter (four feet), pentameter (five feet), hexameter (six feet) and so on.

The combination of foot and meter give birth to various

kinds of rhythm, conveying different emotions and feelings. "Rhythm must have meaning." Ezra Pound ever insisted. (Fussell, 1965: 3) The following are the effects rhythm creates:

Iambic meters can be thoughtful and recollective, since they move from the uncertainty of an unstressed syllable to the certainty of a stressed one.

Trochaic meters, because they start with a stress, can sound assertive.

Dactylic meters tend to be sad. The two unstressed syllables which follow the stress create a feeling of decline, of a falling away from certainty.

Anapaestic meters build up emotional tension by hurrying the reader through unstressed syllables to the stressed one.

With the development of poetry, only iambic pentameter remains the most prevalent poetic line because the iamb sounds like a heart beat. A lot of poems in English, such as Milton's Paradise Lost, Shakespeare's sonnets, are written in the iambic pentameter.

In English, rhyme is also among the effects that poets seeks for, which is defined as "the sameness of sound between words or syllables, especially the ending of lines of a verse, as in day, away; visit, is it; puff, rough." (Hornby, 2002: 1291) Rhyming is important in poems. "When we hear one word rhyme with another, we usually experience pleasure in finding harmony between the two. Harmony creates a feeling of completeness, the sense that something has been resolved or finished." (Gill, 1985: 50) This is particularly true when we expect a rhyme; our ears wait for the rhyming word, and when it comes, we enjoy the feeling that a meaning, a line, or a stanza has been completed. Generally speaking, there are four major forms of rhyme: parallel (AABB); cross rhyme (ABAB); even rhyme (ABCB); and circular rhyme (ABBA).

4.2.2.2 Comparison of empathy in the translation of rhythm and rhyme

When we talk about the musicality or beauty of verses, we usually refer to the rhyme, rhythms and alliteration, assonance, etc. To convey the beauty in sound is to convey the beauty in rhyme and rhythm in the original. And if it is possible for the translator to adopt English words which sound similar to the original, it will be better.

Poetry can hardly be separated totally from music. It is oblivious to the most uninitiated readers that poetry makes a greater use of the "music" of language than does language that is not poetry. The poet chooses words for sound as well as for meaning, and uses the sound as a means of reinforcing meaning. So prominent is this musical quality of poetry that some writers and theorists have made the distinguishing term in their definitions of poetry. In China Liu Xie (刘勰) explained the relationship between poetry and music by saying "poetry is the mind of music and sound is its body"; and a scholar and aesthetician Zhu Guanqian held that "Poetry is pure literature with music." In the west, Edgar Allen Poe described poetry as "music... combined with pleasurable idea"; and T. S. Eliot on occasion even equated his poems to music. (quoted in 刘玉梅, 2004: 50) These prevailing views have illustrated the significance of musical quality in poetry indition and appreciation.

There are two broad ways by which the poet achieves musical quality: by the choice and arrangement of sounds and by the arrangement of accents, in other words, rhyme and rhythm. Yet, different as languages are, how to transpose the musical quality between two discrepant languages is really a challenge for the translator of poetry. (quoted in 刘玉梅, 2004: 50)

1. Conveyance of rhyme

Rhyme is the repetition of the accented vowel sound and all succeeding sounds in important or importantly positioned words; as a rule, this repetition is deliberately made. Rhyme has two main functions. First, it echoes sounds and is thus a source of aesthetic satisfaction. There is pleasure in the sound itself and in the coincidence of sounds, and this pleasure must be associated with the sense of music, of rhythm and beat. Secondly, rhyme assists in the actual structure of verse. (Cuddon, 1979: 573)

Chinese rhyming patterns are different from those in English. Chinese poetry tends to adopts unitary rhyme, while plural rhymes are preferred in English poetry. Chinese character is usually composed of a consonant and a vowel following it. The so-called rhyme in the poetry roughly equals the vowel in pinyin. For example, the Chinese characters "谁" "垂", and "追", have the same vowel, so they are the rhymes. When they are put in the same position of the poetic lines, they rhyme with each other. In classical Chinese poetry usually they are put at the end of the lines. On the contrary, English poems enjoy more freedom in rhyming. They can be rhymed or blank, and can have end rhyme, internal rhyme, or alliteration. Even the rhyme scheme can be various. As is well known, it is not easy to render into English, ancient Chinese poems with full imagery and it is trickier to copy the special rhyme of ancient Chinese poems. Taking such differences into consideration, Professor Xu Yuanchong has proposed to adopt the rhyming patterns which are familiar to English readers in translating Chinese rhymed poetry. Yuan Jinxiang believes that at the time when these translations first appeared in 1917 rhyme was considered the hall-mark of poetry, and there are still people who think that a poetry translator who does not employ rhyme has not done his job. (袁锦翔, 1990)

Most poems in *Hongloumeng* are regulated verses and quatrains, many of which are related to rhymes. Both Yang and Hawkes have endeavoured to convey their beauty in sound by rhyming in different ways.

Example 10:

ST：

彩线难收面上珠，湘江旧迹已模糊。
窗前亦有千竿竹，不识香痕渍也无。

（《红楼梦》第三十四回）

TT1：

No silk thread can string these pearls;
Dim now the tear-stains of those bygone years;
A thousand bamboos grow before my window——
Is each dappled and stained with tears?

(*Yang's translation*)

TT2:

Yet silk preserves but ill the Naiad's tears;
Each salty trace of them fast disappears.
Only the speckled bamboo stems that grow
Outside the window still her tear-marks show.

(*Hawkes' translation*)

The original poem consists of four lines with seven characters in each line and bears the same rhyme at the end of each line, that is "zhu", "hu", "zhu" and "wu". Yang's version has rhyming words in the first two lines as "pearls" and "years", and the last two lines as "window" and "tears", so the rhyme scheme can be described as AABA, which is not so popular among the rhyme schemes listed above in English quatrains;

while in Hawkes' rendition in the first two lines "tears" is rhymed with "disappears", and in the last two lines "grow" rhymes with "show", and the rhyme scheme of the rendition is AABB, which is one of the most popular rhyme schemes in English quatrains and is better than Yang's in reflecting the rhyme beauty. When they are read, comparatively, Hawkes' translation seems to be more moving and leaves us more aftertastes that linger. Both Hawkes' and Yang's dealings still convey in some degree the sound beauty of the original rhyme, but Hawkes' appears to do better in transferring sentiments through the accurate arrangement of rhymes and caters well to the Western readers.

2. Conveyance of rhythm

Rhythm is the movement or sense of movement communicated by the arrangement of stressed and unstressed syllables and by the duration of the syllables. (Cuddon, 1979: 44) Rhythm is an essential of all poetry. Perrine stated that, "rhythm and sound cooperate to produce what we call the music of poetry. This music, as we have pointed out, may serve two general functions: it may be enjoyable in itself; it may be used to reinforce meaning and intensify the communication." (Perrine, 1969)

As is seen in the previous chapters, Chinese and English present quite different features in rhythm pattern. A general principle of translating Chinese rhythm is to find the corresponding rhythmic unit in English, that is, a unit that has the same or similar rhythmic effect of the original. According to Xu Yuanchong, to translate Chinese regulated verses, the translator can try English iambic foot or trochaic foot combined with syllables to convey the rhythm in the original.

Yang Xianyi and Hawkes have also taken the difference into account. From their translations, we can see their different strategies in transferring the original beauty in rhythm.

Example 11:

ST:

参禅偈

你证我证,心证意证。
是无有证,斯可云证。
无可云证,是立足境。
(续)无立足境,方是干净。

(《红楼梦》第二十二回)

TT1:

Should you test me and I test you,
Should heart and mind be tested too,
Till there remained no more to test,
That test would be all of the best.
When nothing can be called a test,
My feet will find a place to rest.

(*Yang's translation*)

TT2:

I swear, you swear.
With heart and mind declare;
But our protest
Is no true test
It would be best
Words unexpected
To understand,
And on that ground.
To take our stand.
But, I perpend,
To have no ground
On which to stand
Were yet more sound.
And there's an end!'

(*Hawkes' translation*)

The above poem is not composed entirely by Lin Daiyu; it is one done with the cooperation of Baoyu and Daiyu. In this chapter, Grandmother Jia arranged a party to celebrate Baochai's birthday. Having enjoyed Beijing Opera, Xiangyun commented that one of the actresses was like Daiyu. Baoyu was afraid that it would annoy Daiyu, so he tried to stop Xiangyun. Unexpectedly, this made both of the two ladies angry. After he came to his own room, he became depressed and could not help crying. In spite of that, he began to study Zhuangzi's thoughts of Inaction. While studying it, he wrote down the first six lines of this poem. Soon after realizing what had happened, Daiyu came into his room and found the poem finished. The next day she shared the poem with Baochai and Xiangyun and invited them to pay a visit to Baoyu together, trying to persuade him to stop idiotic thinking. At this moment, Daiyu told Baoyu that she was dissatisfied with the lines "无可云证，是立足境", stating that the lines were not perfect enough and couldn't be taken as the end of this poem, so Daiyu composed the seventh and eighth lines as a supplement at the end of the poem for the sake of poem's perfection. Then here comes out this Buddhist gatha. From the poem, we can feel the genuine love between Baoyu and Daiyu.

In the ST, each line is made up of four characters, with the rhythm as follows:

你证 — 我证 —
/心证 — 意证 —。
/是 — 无有证 —
/斯可 — 云证 —
/无可 — 云证 —
/是 — 立足境 —。
/(续) 无 —立足境 —
/方是 — 干净 —。

Most pauses in this poem occur after two Chinese characters. All of them end with Chinese characters with falling tones, such as "证"/zhèng/, "境" /jìng/ and "净" /jìng/. The frequent pauses and short sentences together with the ending characters of falling tones bring about a kind of musicality. This kind of rhythm also produces a sense of assertion which expresses Daiyu and Baoyu's deep love with each other.

In the translation, Yang was fully aware of the rhythm in this poem, imitating the original pattern of the poem. Each line of his translation can be divided into tetrameter that is similar to the Chinese four characters, and each line is either iambic or trochaic. If we read the English version, we can easily find the rhythm of this version generates a similar auditory effect in English and the sense of the poem is accordingly reinforced. Furthermore, the end rhyme is perfectly sounded in "you" and "too", "test" and "best", which miraculously mirrors the beauty of the original rhyme and rhythm presented by the repetition of "zheng" and "jing". By contrast, in Hawkes' version, we can find the end rhyme is presented in "sweat" and "declare"; "protest", "test", "best" and "unexpressed"; "understand", "ground" and "stand"; "perpend", "ground", "stand", "sound" and "end", of which the rhythm is not so clear and strong as Yang's, but the advantage of Hawkes' is its shortness and rhyming, which caters for the tone of the original poem and the transfer of Baoyu and Daiyu's moods.

On the whole, Yang Xianyi and Hawkes have translated the poems with rhyme schemes familiar to the English readers, and Yang even tried the English vowels that sound similar to the

Chinese sound. Wang Jun in his MA thesis (2002: 20-26) made a comparative study on rhythm and rhyme for the poetry translation in *Hongloumeng*. It can be found that Yang has frequently changed his style without using the strict-versification, so his rhyme is not so regular. With different numbers of syllables and feet, he has betrayed the rhythmical beauty in the original form. As to Hawkes, he knows well the preference of his readers as well as the tradition of his own language, and thus mainly follows the iambic pentameter and neat rhythm in most of his renderings, which may be more familiar to and easily accepted by the target readers. Therefore, the two translators have used different ways to transfer the sentiments through carefully conveying the beauty in sound. Below are more examples to illustrate their differences,

Example 12:

TT1:

Writing about the Chrysanthemum

Day and / night the / imp of / poetry / assails / men; (11 syllables)

Skirting / the fence/, leaning on / the rock/, they start / chanting; (11)

With the / tip of / the brush/, by the / rime, they / write fine / lines, (13)

Or fa /cing the / moon croon / their sweet / melo / dies. (11)

We may / fill a / page with / sorrow / and self / -pity, (12)

But who / can put / into / words what / autumn / means? (11)

Ever / since Tao / Yuanming / of old / passed ju / dgement (12)

This flow / er's worth / has been / sung through / the cen / turies. (12)

(*Yang's translation*)

TT2:

Celebrating the Chrysanthemums

Down gar / den walks /, in search / of in / spira / tion, (11)
A rest / less de / mon drives / me all / the time; (10)
Then brush / blooms in / to prai /ses , and / the mouth (10)
Grows scud / -sweet, hym / ning those / scents sub /lime. (9)
Yet ea / sier 'twere / a world / of grief / to tell (10)
Than to / lock au / tumn's se / cret in / one rhyme. (10)
That mi / racle old / Tao did / once a / ttain; (9)
Since when / a thou / sand bards / have tried / in vain (10)

(*Hawkes' translation*)

Example 13:

TT1:

Before / the drin / king starts /, ere / poems are / made (11 syllables)

He goes / to the / Fairy / Isles in / search of / spring, as/ king a / boon. (15)

Not in / quest of / dew from / the Bod / hisatt/ va's kun / di, (13)

But to / beg a / plum branch / by the / fence of / the Go/ ddess of / the Moon. (16)

He re / turns to / earth with / a load / of cold / red snow, (12)

A frag / rant cloud / but far / from the / dusty / world; (11)

Its for / ked boughs / resting / on the / poet's slim / shoulders. (12)

His clothes / by moss / from the / nunne / ry still / purled. (11)

(*Yang's translation*)

TT2:

Asking for the Red Plum

Wine not / yet broached / nor ver / ses yet /composed (10)

In quest / of spring / I sped / to E / lysium (10)

Twas not / the balm / from Guan / yin's vase / I craved (10)

Across / that thresh / old, but / her flowe / ring plum (10)

A fro / zen world / ling, for / red flowers / I begged; (10)

The saint / cut frag / rant clouds / and gave / me some. (10)

Pity / my verse / so an / gular / and thin. (10)

(*Hawkes' translation*)

4.2.3 Aesthetic empathy in term of form

4.2.3.1 Definition of poetic form

Probably the most conspicuous distinction of poetry compared with other literary types is its special form. Beauty in sound pleases the ear while beauty in form pleases the eye. Formal elements also make sense and add much poetic effect to poetry. Just as Louis Macneice said, "In any poet's poem the shape is half the meaning." (quoted in Fussell, 1965: 133) By form we include line length, verse pattern, repetition of words, parallelism in structure, etc. The first entry of the interpretations for form in the *Longman Dictionary* (1995) is "shape; outward appearance". A poem's visual pattern should be appreciated by the readers, the effects of typography and stanza shapes are used to enhance a poem's meaning and to create an effect. These effects, like those achieved by painters and sculptors, can be extremely powerful because of their physicality. Some poems seem to ask to be thought of as visual objects first. Poetic form, as Wang Hongchao (王洪超, 1999: 8) defined it, refers to its phonology and graphology, its use of words and phrases with rich connotations and high literalness, its irregular word order at the level of syntax, and its use of all kinds of rhetorical devices at the level of semantics. In all, they constitute the main extrinsic features of poetry.

Chinese poems are beautiful in their agreed form, presenting themselves apparently as squares or circles, which, to some extent, satisfy the aesthetic psychology need of the Chinese people, who hope to pursue the perfection. In the Chinese eye, both squares and circles are symbols of perfection and regularity.

A poet will impose poetry not only an internal order in material, image, concept, logic and sound but also an external order in structure or form in the hope of giving it not only an inside logical order but also an outside symmetry. The beauty in form is indispensable. On the one hand, it embodies the ideal of the work; on the other hand, it materializes the artistic concept and sentiments of the poet. Some critics even hold that what makes a poem a poem is not what it has said, and that the total meaning of a poem is partly implied in its structure and form. So translators must take the form into account besides sense and sound in translation.

4.2.3.2 Evolution and differences of Chinese and English poetic form

Great changes have taken place in poetic form throughout history. As a result, we are left with a number of kinds of verse form. Wang Guowei gave his comment in *Renjian China*, "When a literary form has been current for a long time and used by many, it naturally becomes hackneyed. So, four-word-line verse, having lost its freshness, gave place to the Ch'u tz'u, which in turn gave place to five-word-line verse; and when that has lost its freshness, it gave place to seven-word-line verse. When ancient-style verse lost its freshness, it gave place to regulated verse and quatrains, and these in turn gave place to tz'u." (王洪超, 1999: 9) Each poetic form is marked by its distinct features of that time.

In ancient times, there was no line-break in Chinese poetry, but the inerratic rhyme functioned as marks of line-break. Later, the arrayal in lines has definitely made the beauty in form of Chinese poetry more visible. There are four major types of classical Chinese poetry. Old style poem (gu shi) contains four characters in each line and all the poems were written before the Tang Dynasty. Regulated verse (lü shi) is a very popular form of poetry in Tang Dynasty, which has eight lines, each consisting of characters in fixed five or seven numbers in each line. Jue ju is a shorter type of regulated verse which has only four lines. They all provide a visual beauty of neatness and harmony. Then, some poets broke the norm and created Song lyric that is another most famous type of classical Chinese poetry in the Song Dynasty. Unlike the regulated poetry, the numbers of characters are not identical in each line. However, in the West, it has been taken for granted that poetry should have line-breaks since ancient times. In general, there are three general kinds of form into which a Western poet may cast his work: continuous form, stanzaic form, and fixed form. Poetry in the continuous form has no fixed structure, its stanza-dividing depends on the thought just like a prose. Stanzaic form refers to a series of stanzas, which are repetitive units with fixed number of lines, the same rhythm pattern and the same pattern of rhyming words. Fixed form is a traditional pattern used in a whole poem, such as limerick and sonnet which are widely used in English poetry. Generally speaking, lines with over ten syllables are more often found in English poetry.

The difference in forms is so great between Chinese and English classical poetry that it is difficult to translate these two languages into each other, in particular, from Chinese into English. Lǔ Shuxiang said, "The use of antithesis is advocated in Chinese poems, while there is hardly any antithesis in English poems but sentences divided into several lines. When dealing with the antitheses in Chinese poems, some translators may strive to translate it sentence by sentence, aiming at transferring the neatness in form; some may turn it into sentences divided into several lines." (quoted in 张毅, 2007: 75) Comparatively speaking, in order to convey the beauty in the forms of Chinese poetry, translators should keep the same number of lines and almost the same length of each line as those of the original poem. For example, a quatrain is usually translated into four lines, and a regulated verse is usually rendered into eight lines. In Chinese poems, the number of vowels in a line indicates the number of words. In English, a syllable is the basic unit to signify word length. There is always more than one syllable in a word. In

Chinese-English translation, we often have to use eight to ten syllables a line to indicate what is indicated by five Chinese characters a line, and twelve syllables a line to indicate what is indicated by seven Chinese characters a line. Of course, it is not an absolute rule.

4.2.3.3 Conveyance of the "beauty in form"

In traditional Chinese poetry, especially in regulated verses, antithetical couples are quite common, which can produce a sort of symmetrical beauty. The following two lines in《离尘歌》have the same number of Chinese characters with the same part of speech. Yang and Hawkes have managed to translate the couplet into the following:

Example 14:

ST:

我所居兮，青梗之峰；
我所游兮，鸿蒙太空。

（《红楼梦》第一百二十回）

TT1:

My home is Blue Ridge Peak,
I roam the primeval void.

(*Yang's translation*)

TT2:

On Greensickness Peak

I dwell;
In the Cosmic void
I roam.

(*Hawkes' translation*)

It can be seen that in Yang's translation, he retains the form and flavor of Chinese poems, and employs the normal order and complete sentences in the entire poem, without any rhyming at all, while in Hawkes', inversions are properly applied for the purpose of enhancing the steepness of the English poem arrangements.

The poem *the Song of Flower-Burial* (《葬花吟》) (For full text, see Example 8.) is made up of fifty-two lines with remarkable end-rhymes. In addition, as a poem of ancient style, this poem has seven characters in most of its lines except the 16th, 39th and 40th lines. While reading it, a reader with a rich fund of ancient Chinese may be consciously or unconsciously aware of the beauty in form. Both Yang and Hawkes retain the original form in most cases, and translate it into English stanzaic form, organizing clearly the poem into thirteen stanzas in which each has four lines. Hawkes translate forty - seven lines into ten syllables, only three lines into nine syllables and two lines into eleven syllables, which makes his version as neat and tidy as the original. By contrast, Yang pays more attention to the rhyme scheme and adopts rhyming words at the end of each even-numbered line. Thus a clearer visual effect is achieved in the

English translation. In this sense, his English translation has conveyed the original beauty in form directly and visibly to the readers. However, the structure of Yang's version is loose, for he translates the lines mostly into seven to fourteen syllables:

Example 15:

ST:

花谢花飞花满天，红消香断有谁怜？
游丝软系飘春榭，落絮轻沾扑绣帘。

（《红楼梦》第二十七回）

TT1:

As blossoms fade and fly across the sky,
Who pities the faded red, the scent that has been?
Softly the gossamer floats over spring pavilions,
Gently the willow fluff wafts to the embroidered screen.

(*Yang's translation*)

TT2:

The blossoms fade and falling fill the air,
Of fragrance and bright hues bereft and bare.
Floss drifts and flutters round the Maiden's bower,
Or softly strikes against her curtained door.

(*Hawkes' translation*)

Chapter Five
Comparison of Cultural Empathy in Poetry Translation in *Hongloumeng*

"To understand, appreciate, and respect cultural differences is central to all practical treatments of intercultural communication."

——Milton J. Bennett

As is known, language and culture are closely connected. On the one hand, language is the carrier of culture; without language culture would not be possible. That's to say, we use language to convey ideas and beliefs. We exchange and create facts, experience, and events through language. We know about and learn culture via language. Language is the significant way by which we conduct our social lives. On the other hand, language is influenced and shaped by culture. It reflects culture and reinforces culture in turn. To some extent, people can see culture through language. Each language corresponds with a particular culture. Malinowski made the most powerful argument by saying directly that "an understanding of the language was impossible without constantly relating it to the culture in which it was operative." (quoted in Ogden and Richards, 1923: 305)

5.1 Culture, language, translation and their mutual relationship

Wang Zuoliang has emphasized the cultural importance in translation repeatedly, and once remarked "The greatest difficulty in translation lies in the differences between two cultures. What is self-evident in one culture has to be painstakingly explained in another culture." (quoted in袁锦祥, 1992: 27. The translation is mine.) Wang Zuoliang also pointed out that "a translator must be 'a cultural ambassador'. What he deals with is individual words, and what he faces is two different cultures." (王佐良, 1990: 19. The translation is mine.) Nida presented the similar view: "The role of language within a culture and the influence of the culture on the meanings of words and idioms are so pervasive that scarcely any text can be adequately understood without careful consideration of its cultural background." (Nida, 2001b: i) These proposals show the important role that culture plays in translation. Culture is such a complex concept that it is difficult to pin down. Generally there are two ways to define culture: in a broad sense and in a narrow sense. In a narrow sense, culture is confined to intellectual and conceptual areas. A good example of an all-inclusive and descriptive definition in a broad sense is the one advanced by Daniel Bates and Fred Plog: "Culture is a system of shared beliefs, values, customs, behaviors, and artifacts that members of a society use to cope with their world and with one another, and that are transmitted from generation to generation through learning," which includes not only patterns of behavior but also patterns of thought (shared meanings that members of a society attach to various phenomena, natural and intellectual, including religion and ideologies), artifacts (tools, pottery, houses, machines, works of art), and the culturally transmitted skills and techniques used to make the artifacts. In this thesis, culture is considered in its broad sense. As defined by some scholars, Nida defined culture succinctly as "the totality of beliefs and practices of a society." (Nida, 2001b: 105) Peter Newmark described culture as "the way of life and its manifestations that are peculiar to a community that uses a particular language as its means of expression." (Newmark, 2001: 94)

Language is the use by human beings of voice sounds, and often written symbols representing these sounds, in organized combinations and patterns in order to express and communicate thoughts and feelings. (*American Heritage Dictionary of the English Language*)

From the definitions above, we can see that language is part of culture — part of spiritual wealth created by mankind, and it has common characteristics with culture — it is used by people with a shared history or set of traditions. Every nation has its own culture and can find its expressions directly in language.

Translation means the act or process of translating,

especially from one language into another language. It is an important form of linguistic performance, an effective means of communication between people belonging to different speech communities. It begins with language and ends with language. Yet "it involves two different cultures instead of two languages because it takes the form of language but aims to exchange and communicate different cultures. Culture is the soil on which language exists and the object that language reflects." (徐丹, 1998: 3. The translation is mine.) Translations are not made in a vacuum. Translators function in a given culture at a given time. The way they understand themselves and their culture is one of the factors that they may influence the way in which they translate. Those who have not reflected on the translation process, and especially those who have not themselves attempted literary translation (and in particular the translation of poetry), frequently think of it as essentially the moving of words from one language to another. The notion of literal translation, plainly, is founded on some such conceptions. If all languages were simply a matter of words arranged in strings, then of course it would be relatively easy—given acknowledged differences in available vocabulary—to transpose the language strings of one tongue into the language strings of another. Surely, translation is nothing like that easy. (Raffel, 1988: 51)

5.2 Application of the approach of cultural empathy in literary translation

Literary translation calls for not only the technological change in its external form from one language to another, but also the translator's profound understanding of the creative process of the author through the tool of the original language. During the process of translation, through cultural empathy, the translator can consciously surpass the framework of his native culture and thoroughly comprehend the culture of the target language in order to experience the psychological process of the original culture and reason out the closest equivalents in his own ideas about life and life experiences. Then through the use of another literary language, he can properly reproduce the artistic images and writing styles of the original works and provide the readers of the translated works with the same enlightenment, touch and aesthetic enjoyment of the readers of the original works.

Literary works as a complicated artistic whole with rich and colorful contents, range from one's interior monologue, one's instantaneous feeling, a marvelous war picture, a poetical love story, the epitome of the whole society, to odd portrayal of life. No matter what kind it is, "sentiment" is present in every part of literary works. Sentiment belongs to an aesthetic catalogue, and one of the most active elements in cultural psychology, which should not be ignored in literary translation. As Liu Xie (刘勰) pointed out "故情者,文之经,辞者,理之纬" in *Emotion and Hunting: the Literary Mind and the Carving of Dragons* (文心雕龙·情采). Thus, the transference of sentiment is as important as that of sense in translation. In addition, with distinctive cultural colors and connotations, "sentiment" itself is a link of cultural form, so it mustn't be abandoned during the process of translation. Only by reading and re-constructing the original world, grasping the structure and contents of the works, and having a thorough understanding of the author's intention, attitude and the characters' emotional world in the works, can the translator achieve the closest equivalents to the original text, and be personally on the scene with the readers. A lot of literary works states its feelings frankly, while in most cases, they remain submerged or half-hidden. In this regard, an excellent translator always understands the original works, experiences the original so as to attain imagic, concrete and perceptual characteristics, then observes and imagines the images, finds out the emotional connection with the readers, finally re-experiences and re-constructs the original cultural world and creates the translator's world that is similar to or the same as the original.

For example: 白日依山尽,黄河入海流。欲穷千里目,更上一层楼。(王之涣《登鹳雀楼》)(quoted in 李晓红,2006:76)

TT1:

The sun behind the western hills glows, / and toward the sea the Yellow River Flows. / Wish you an endless view to cheer your eyes? / Then one more story mount and higher rise.

TT2:

The setting sun behind the mountains glows, / the muddy Yellow River Seawards flows. / If more distant views are what you desire, / you simply climb up a storey higher.

TT3:

Ling's ring is the setting sun about the mountain height, / surging is the Yellow River towards the vast sea. / Aim higher and up the tower take another flight, / to acquire a vision broader than one thousand li.

This is a very famous Tang Poem. The third and the fourth lines in TT1 meaning "你想一睹无限风光、一饱眼福吗？那就再登一层楼、再爬高些吧！" fail to reproduce the subjective consciousness as if these words come from a guide. "Muddy Yellow River" in TT2 is rendered in the context of the poet's "absence"; and the third and fourth line meaning "如果你想看得更远些，只要再爬高一些就行" have the flow similar to TT1, which is caused by the void of affect intervention to the poet. The translator of TT3 empathizes with the love for country, rivers and mountains and the spirit of striving, uses imagination to put the "sun" and "Yellow River" in front of him, and dates back to the poet's aesthetic experience. In the meantime, an inverted sentence is used in Line One and Two, accompanied by the expressive words such as "lingering" and "surging". Line Three and Line Four are imperatives which apply to everyone; "aim higher" refers to high aim corresponding with the original meaning of "climbing the tower"; "vision" and "another flight" carry the characteristics of symbolism and deep meanings. Hence, TT3 is more skillful than others.

Since culture is inclusive of everything, which is a whole system of human knowledge, beliefs and behaviors, the multifaceted nature of culture and communication makes it difficult to arrive at a single definition of culture. A translator is supposed to be a "real cultural man" to cultivate his own intercultural consciousness and know more about the source culture, not only an excellent source language commander, but also familiar with its geography, economy, history, custom, philosophical thoughts, technological advances and sentimentality and so on. As Lu Xun once remarked, "The purpose of real translation is firstly to read foreign works extensively, which needs empathy as well as an increase in wisdom." (quoted in 李晓红, 2006: 77. The translation is mine.) At the same time, he should be a master of his national culture, which makes it possible to empathize. This is illustrated below:

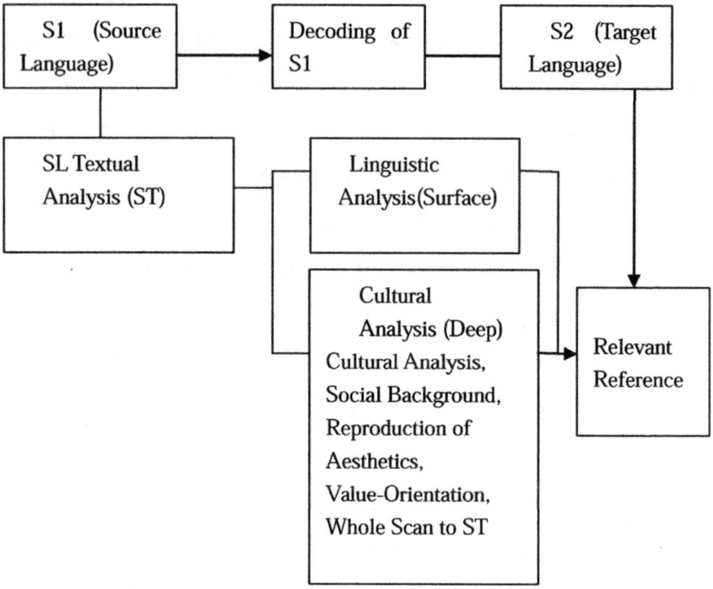

Figure 5.1 Diagram of Cultural Encoding

5.3 Realization of the approach of cultural empathy in literary translation

Literary translation involves a great diversity of knowledge of literature, art, culture and history, and a literary translator lives in a certain cultural environment deeply branded by the culture. Excellent translation should be the artistic reproduction of the original rather than word-for-word translation or inflexible transformation. With the aid of empathy, a translator is capable of finding out the hidden cultural connotation in order to arrive at similarity in spirit, even in sublimation.

Cross-cultural awareness refers to the cross-cultural communication among participants on the cultural sensitivity of the cognitive factors. Robert Hanvey divides cross-cultural awareness into four levels:

At Level I are those who can be aware of superficial or very visible cultural traits of other cultures. The first level uses information about the "other" culture to create superficial stereotypes.

At Level II are those who have been aware of, through either direct or secondhand experience, cultural traits that significantly contrast with one's own practice. The second level is based on an expanded knowledge of the "other" culture that focuses on its differences, and the subsequent difficulties it presents.

At Level III are those who accept the "other" culture at an intellectual level and use it as a frame of reference for understanding. It makes sense to them.

Finally, at the fourth level, empathy of the "other" culture is achieved through direct experience. This is an indispensable skill for people moving out of traditional settings. The people who have this level of cross-cultural awareness can know how another culture feels from the standpoint of the insider. Ideally, that means getting inside the heads of those strangers and looking out at the world through their eyes. Then anything strange becomes familiar and totally believable.

Although cross-cultural awareness is hard to realize, Hanvey thinks that cultural empathy can be achieved. What's more, a translator has to cultivate his aesthetic awareness which means the sensitivity of beauty.

Actually, empathy in literary translation is a changeable process of experience, transformation, construction and creation. Firstly, the translator makes a scanning-like analysis, judgement and reasoning of TL attainments (vocabulary, grammar, style and rhetoric), implied cultural knowledge and ST language structure so as to infer the aesthetic components of the original features. Then, a process of emotional communication surmounting space and time exists between the author and the translator, the translator is obliged to break the fetters of his own cultural tradition and enter the original world. Finally, the translator has to experience an artistic re-creative process, reveal the flitting and errant artistic image arriving at not only linguistic equivalence but also empathy with each other. Certainly, it is a hard process. If compared to free dancing, translation is just dancing in handcuffs and shackles, even more gracefully. It is because the literary translator shouldn't be left entirely to his own imagination unconstrained or unbounded, wantonly display his own artistic talents or personality, but should follow the author's every train of thought, try to figure out the author's thinking, so that his re-creation forever can't surpass the author's direction.

Bennett has proposed a six-step model on how to achieve cultural empathy, which is a guide to the sequential development of empathic skills. Each step is a necessary condition to the next. (Bennett, 1998: 209-212)

Step One: Assuming Difference

In contrast to the assumption that all people are basically similar, we could assume that each human being is essentially unique. If we accept that we might be different, given different constructions and circumstances, then we are free to imagine our thoughts and feelings from that different perspective.

Step Two: Knowing self

The preparation called for is to know ourselves sufficiently well so that an easy reestablishment of individual identity is possible. If we are aware of our own cultural and individual values, assumptions, and beliefs, that is, how we define our identities, then we need not fear losing those selves.

Step Three: Suspending Self

One way of thinking about this procedure is to imagine that the self, or identity, is an arbitrary boundary that we draw between ourselves and the rest of the world, including other people.

Step Four: Allowing Guided Imagination

For accurate interpersonal empathy to occur, we must allow our imagination to be guided into the experience of a specific other person. If we are successful in allowing our imagination to be captured by the other person, we are in the position to imaginatively participate in that person's experience.

Step Five: Allowing Empathic Experience

When we have allowed our imagination to be guided inside the other person, we are in the position to experience that person as if that person were ourselves. With empathy, and only with empathy, we are privileged to live briefly in the least accessible land of all-another person's experience.

Step Six: Reestablishing Self

The reestablishment of self is a necessary component of empathic communication. The failure to do so eventuates in a diffusion of identity, or ego-loss. Interpersonal empathy allows the controlled and temporary suspension of identity for a particular purpose-the understanding of another person. When this purpose is achieved, the boundaries of self are best reinstituted.

5.4 Comparison of cultural empathy in poetry translation in *Hongloumeng*

The present thesis classifies culture into five systems following Nida's classification: ecological culture, material culture, social culture, religious culture, linguistic culture. Now let's have a look at the different translation of the poetry in *Hongloumeng* from the point of view of Nida's five aspects of culture.

5.4.1 Comparison of empathy in terms of ecological culture

Ecology is a branch of biology that deals with the habits of living things, especially their relation to their environment. (Oxford Dictionary, 1992: 372)

Ecological culture refers to the culture related with the situated area, natural environment and geographical features of a given area. It includes plants, living creatures and surrounding. Culture is formed and developed in a special ecological environment. People's cognition of the nature is different because they live in distinctive geographical locations and different environments, which results in different cultures. The geographical diversity and peculiarity get reflected in the languages concerned, so the expressions will become diverse and peculiar. Usually the names of those plants and animals peculiar to an area can only be found in the language spoken in this area. For example, "many countries have "local" words for plains — 'prairies', 'veld', 'tundras', 'pampas', 'savannahs', 'llanos'—all with strong elements of local color. Geographical features can be normally distinguished from other cultural terms in that they are usually value-free, politically and commercially." (Newmark, 2001: 96) Even for the same natural phenomenon, different cultures may invest it with different cognition, understanding or aesthetic conceptions. As for translation, the uniqueness of ecological culture is likely to lead to lexical gap or vagueness which gives rise to translation problems. Among the poetry in *Hongloumeng*, cultural elements with ecological features are most pervasively employed by Cao Xueqin. These ecological features are combined with the literary tradition, custom or ethical psychology; as a result, the translation problems become much trickier. There exist certain ecological features so peculiar or unknown that they may not be understood denotatively or figuratively, when translated literally.

Example 16:

ST:

爱彼之貌容兮，香培玉琢；
美彼之态度兮，凤翥龙翔.

（《红楼梦》第五回）

TT1:

Sweet her face, compact of fragrance, carved in jade;
and she bears herself like **a phoenix** or **dragon** in flight.

(*Yang's translation*)

TT2:

I wonder at her fine-cut featured—
Marble, which fragrance marks as one with living creatures;
And I admire her queenly gait,
Like stately dance of **simurgh** with his mate.

(*Hawkes' translation*)

Yang is faithful to the cultural image of the original text, rendering "凤" and "龙" into "phoenix" and "dragon" semantically.

However, in English-speaking countries, phoenix is said to be a bird born in the Arabic desert in the legend, which, after living for about five or six hundred years, burns itself into ashes with its wings fanning the flames and then revives. So "phoenix" connotes the receiving and revival. "Dragon" in the Western legend is said to be a huge lizard with long wings and tail and scales all over, whose mouth can spray fire; in the stories of the Bible, it is the symbol of "evilness and crimes", as Satan is called the great dragon. Accordingly if you describe someone as a dragon, he will be offended, and if you call a woman a dragon, you mean that she is extremely fierce and unpleasant. On the contrary, in Chinese people's heart, "凤" is a symbol of dignity, peace, fortune and nobleness, while "龙" has been given a high status among all animals and enjoys a good reputation, and it is something sacred and the Chinese people proudly regard "龙" as the ancestor of the Chinese nation. That's why the Chinese call themselves "龙的传人" (descendants of the dragon) and the Chinese feudal emperors were often referred to as "真龙天子". The Chinese people dance with dragon lanterns, and hold dragon-boat races on traditional festivals in the hope for good luck and prosperity. Here, Hawkes omits the Chinese cultural information of "凤" and "龙", rendering them into "simurgh", a monstrous bird of Persian legend, imagined as rational, having the power of speech, and of great age. Thus it seems to be inappropriate to transfer the sentiments in the original and the information to be transferred is ruined, because of his intention of being empathetic to the readers. Meanwhile Hawkes seems to be weaker in understanding the sense of the original. On the contrary, Yang retained the cultural image of the original one, which aroused different images to the Western readers, arriving at being empathetic towards the author.

Example 17:

ST:

枉自温柔和顺,空云似桂如兰

（《红楼梦》第五回）

TT1:

Nothing avail her gentleness and compliance,
Osmanthus and **orchid** with her fragrance vie;

(*Yang's translation*)

TT2:

What price your kindness and compliance
Of **sweetest flower** the rich perfume?

(*Hawkes' translation*)

"桂" and "兰" are two aromatic flowers, which are often used figuratively in Chinese poetry to describe a woman's fragrance and liveliness, which may be familiar to Chinese readers. Yang tries to preserve the flower in the target text. Although the usage of "桂" and "兰" in Chinese poetry may seem strange to the target addressees, they can infer its connotation knowing the fragrance of these two flowers. Hence both inter -textual coherence and intra-textual coherence have been achieved successfully. On the contrary, Hawkes renders these two flowers as "sweetest flower" in an attempt to directly offer the readers the connotation of "桂" and "兰" used in the original. So Yang is better in accurate sense translation than Hawkes and transfers the sentiments in the original better.

Example 18:

ST:

松影一庭惟见鹤,梨花满地不闻莺

（《红楼梦》第二十三回）

TT1:

Only **a stork** can be seen in the pine-shadowed court,

No oriole sings in the snow which has drifted like **pear-blossom**.

(*Yang' translation*)

TT2:

Only a **stork** outside is to be found

No orioles now, though **white flowers** mask the ground.

(*Hawkes' translation*)

The poem reflects the nobles' elegant leisure. On the deep

night of chilly peaceful winter, the waiter made tea with newly-cleaned snow. The author used "松" and "鹤" together to create a peaceful image in reader's minds, and compared "梨花" to snow although "松" or "鹤" didn't exist in the real situation. Despite the fact that "松" and "鹤" are ecologically familiar to both Chinese and English readers, the imagery in the poem may seem strange to the latter. Hawkes rendered "梨花" into "white flowers", so in his translation he had not fully considered the context of the original and made his version less accurate than Yang's. In this way, the sentiments in the original may not be well expressed in translation.

Britain is an island country, where fishery and ocean shipping have played a very important part in its development, so the difference of geographical position between Britain and China may arouse differences in the English and the Chinese language. Close attention should be paid when translating expressions related to environment. In many poems of *Hongloumeng*, these two phrases "东风" and "西风" are employed more than once, for example,

Example 19:

ST:

对立东风里，主人应解怜。

（《红楼梦》第十八回）

TT1:

Facing each other in the soft **east wind,**

They surely bring their mistress peace of mind.

(*Yang's translation*)

TT2:

Their Mistress, standing in soft **summer breeze,**

Finds quiet content in everything she sees.

(*Hawkes' translation*)

Example 20:

ST:

莫向东风怨别离。

(《红楼梦》第二十二回)

Blames not **the east wind** for this separation.

(*Yang's translation*)

TT2:

And on **the wind** I drift off broken hearted.

(*Hawkes' translation*)

Example 21:

ST:

怅望西方抱闷思。

(《红楼梦》第三十八回)

TT1:

I gaze around in **the west wind**, sick at heart.

(*Yang's translation*)

TT2:

The autumn wind that through the knotgrass blows.

(*Hawkes' translation*)

From the above renderings, we find that Yang has replaced "东风" with "east wind" and "西风" with "west wind", while Hawkes has replaced them respectively with "summer breeze", "the wind" and "the autumn wind". Due to different geographical locations of China and Britain, "东风" and "西风" stand for different connotations in Chinese and English. As China is located in East Asia, faces the Pacific Ocean which brings warm, humid air in both spring or summer, Chinese people often associate the east wind with warmth and comfort. And the west wind means a cold and desolate wind in the disconsolate chilly autumn or winter. Conversely, the east wind can only bring Great Britain, located in Western Europe, and facing the Atlantic Ocean, freezing cold and dampness. And the west wind is to be welcomed as warm and agreeable. Therefore British people dislike the east wind, they like the west wind, which represents warmth and spring. There are two famous sentences from Shelley's *Ode to the West Wind*: O, "wind, if winter comes, can spring be far behind?" Here, "wind" should be understood as "西风", or else it will bring about confusion to Chinese readers who are unfamiliar with the regional difference.

Here in this case "东风" and "西风" have become a cultural phenomenon associated with the psychology of the

Chinese and the British. Yang preserves such cultural information as an endeavor to reproduce the spirit of the original poem on the basis of the author's intention in the ST, empathizing to the author and ST. As for Hawkes' version, the English readers will have the same response with that of the Chinese after reading it. He tried his best to make his translation close to the English readers and to pave the way for them. So he is empathizing to the readers who are unfamiliar with the Chinese culture to ease their reading burden.

5.4.2 Comparison of empathy in terms of material culture

The term "material culture" is often used by archaeologists as a non-specific way to refer to the artifacts or other concrete things left by past cultures. Divergent living conditions, lifestyles and habits produce some peculiar objects or utensils owned by certain nations. As time went on, these utensils evolve into various cultural symbols. Newmark categorized it into four parts: food, clothes, houses and town, and transport. (Newmark, 2001: 95) Material culture covers a wide range from food, clothes, house, transport, handicrafts to ways of production, exchange and many other things all of which are culturally loaded and without which life, commerce, agriculture and industry could not be conducted. In the case of *Hongloumeng*, the translation problems prove to be far more complicated as a result of the great differences between Chinese and English material culture. Since *Hongloumeng* as an encyclopedia is such a refined, extensive and profound classic composed in the Qing Dynasty that it's not easy to identify some of the materials specific for that period for the modern Chinese readers, let alone the English readers who are in another culture. In the following examples, how the translation problems are solved by the two translators will be examined.

Example 22:

ST:

好了歌解

陋室空堂,当年笏满床。
衰草枯杨. 曾为歌舞场。
蛛丝儿结满雕梁,绿纱今又糊在蓬窗上。
说什么脂正浓、粉正香,如何两鬓又成霜?
昨日黄土垅头埋白骨,今宵红灯帐底卧鸳鸯。
金满箱,银满箱,展眼乞丐人皆谤。
正叹他人命不长,那知自己归来丧!
训有方,保不定日后做强梁。
择膏粱,谁承望流落在烟花巷!
因嫌纱帽小,致使锁枷扛;
昨怜破袄寒,今嫌紫蟒长。
……

(《红楼梦》第一回)

TT1:

Mean huts and empty halls
Where **emblems of nobility** once hung;
Dead weeds and withered trees,
Where men have once danced and sung.
Carved beams are swathed in cobwebs
But briar-choked casements screened again with gauze;
While yet the rouge is fresh, the powder fragrant,
The hair at the temples turns hoary-for what cause?
Yesterday, yellow clay received white bones;
Today, red lanterns light the love-birds' nest;
While men with gold and silver by the chest
Turn beggars, scorned by all and dispossessed.
A life cut short one moment makes one sigh,
Who would have known it's her turn next to die?
No matter with what pains he schools his sons,
Who knows if they will turn to brigandry?
A pampered girl brought up in luxury
May slip into a quarter of ill fame;
Resentment at **a low official rank**
May lead to fetters and a felon's shame.
In ragged coat one shivered yesterday,
Today a purple robe he frowns upon.

(*Yang' translation*)

TT2:

Mean hovels and abandoned halls
Where **courtiers** once paid daily calls:
Bleak haunts where weeds and willows scarcely thrive, were once with mirth and revelry alive.
Whilst cobwebs shroud the mansion's gilded beams, the cottage casement with choice muslin gleams.
Would you of perfumed elegance recite?
Even as you speak, the raven locks turn white.
Who yesterday her lord's bones laid in clay,
On silken bridal-bed shall lie today.
Coffers with gold and silver filled:
Now, in a trice, a tramp but all reviled.
One at some otter's short life gives a sigh,
Not knowing that he, too, goes home-to die!
The sheltered and well-educated lad,
In spite of all you care, may turn out bad;
And the delicate, fastidious maid
End in a foul stews, playing a shameful trade.
The judge whose **hat** is too small for his head
Wears, in the end, a convict's cangue instead.
Who shivering once in rags bemoaned his fate,
Today finds fault with scarlet robes of state.

(*Hawkes' translation*)

The first two lines describe the scenery that is tricky to

render, because some activities are involved in it. "笏" in the first line is a word unique to Chinese culture; it refers to a tablet held before the breast by officials when received in audience by the emperor, which is hard to find during the contemporary era. Hawkes translated the sentence "当年笏满床" into "where courtiers once paid daily calls"(曾是朝臣们每日上朝之地), successfully transferring from scene to events so as to add creativity and vividness, so that we can experience the scene in those years, while Yang translated it into "where emblems of nobility once hung" (曾悬挂着贵族的徽饰). Both avoid translating it into "满床的笏" directly and conveyed the implication as a whole, so that it is not difficult for the westerners to understand the Chinese cultural connotation of "笏满床". Therefore both of the two translators have satisfactorily empathized to the English readers. Another term is "纱帽", which originally refers to the black gauze cap worn by feudal officials and now denotes official position. Here, Yang and Hawkes rendered it into "a low official rank" (官位低) and "whose hat is too small for his head" (他的头帽子太小) respectively. It's obvious that Yang reserves the cultural connotation; on the contrary Hawkes was unable to apprehend the deep implication that it was mistranslated. The context implies "纱帽小" is not because the hat is too small for his head, but because the rank is low. It can be concluded that Yang is better at reproducing the spirit of the ST.

Example 23:

ST:

秋夜即事

绛云轩里绝喧哗，桂魄流光浸茜纱。

苔锁石纹容睡鹤，井飘桐露湿栖鸦。

抱衾婢至舒金凤，倚槛人归落翠花。

静夜不眠因酒渴，沉烟重拨索烹茶。

（《红楼梦》第二十三回）

TT1:

Autumn Night

The red pavilion scented with rue is hushed,

Moonlight floods the gauze dyed with madder;

Crows asleep by the well are wet with dew from the plane tree,

And storks roost on mossy boulders,

A maid spreads the gold-phoenix quilt,

The girl coming back from the balcony drops her trinkets;

Sleepless at night and thirsty after wine

I relight the incense and call for **fresh tea.**

(*Yang's translation*)

TT2:

Autumn

In Red Rue Study, far from worldly din,

Through rosy gauze moonlight comes flooding in.

Outside, a stork sleeps on moss-wrinkled rocks,
And dew from well-side trees the crow's wings soaks.
A maid the great quilt's golden bird has spread;
Her languid master droops his raven head.
Wine-parched and sleepless, in the still night he cries
For **tea**, and soon thick smoke and steam arise.

(*Hawke's translation*)

China is the homeland of tea. It's believed that China had tea shrubs as early as 5, 000 to 6, 000 years ago, and human cultivation of tea plants dates back at least 2,000 years. Chinese have been sipping tea for over 2,000 years—ever since the Han Dynasty and every dynastic period has introduced refinements in tea making methods and material. Since time immemorial, tea has been the major drink of the Chinese people and has been indispensable in their life. Tea, in the past, was admired by the upper-classes for its pure and elegant quality. Tea-tasting was considered a refined cultural activity and artistic preoccupation for Chinese literati and officialdom. Tea and tea-related activities have penetrated various aspects of social life and take on unique cultural characteristics.

In Chapter 23 of *Hongloumeng*, there are a few poems related with tea. In the above poem, the poet put the sleepless night's love and feelings in autumn into vivid description, and Jai Baoyu's noble character with nothing crave temporarily showed clearly. "茶" and "酒" depend on and interact with each other, both of which reveal the poet's connotation most incisively and vividly. Yang put both "茶" and "酒" at the end of the sentence and "烹茶" is nominalized as "fresh tea", making the freshness and purity stand out, which is in accordance with the Chinese cultural tradition of "wine" and "tea" mentioned in the same breath. Although the process of tea-making is lost, Yang did well in the transference of sentiments with "wine" and "tea" placed together creatively along with the amplication of "fresh tea", therefore, empathized accurately towards the original poet. As a result, the artistic realm of ST and TT is well matched. It can be assumed that the target readers interested in Chinese tea culture can appreciate the charm of the cultural image from the marvelous TT; while Hawkes paid more attention to the language culture and the target reader of the TL and the capacity of culture is considered more, so he adopted the inter-contextual information pertaining to the culture and literature of the TL.

China is a country with a long history of wine culture as well as tea culture. Wine plays a very important part in the everyday life of the ancient Chinese and seems to be a basic necessity in the life of the Chinese people across social classes on both casual and formal occasions of private or public gatherings, banquets and sacrifices. *Hongloumeng*, as "the encyclopedia of the terminal Chinese feudal society" is a novel full of descriptions about wine culture which is depicted in 56 chapters of *Hongloumeng* 251 times. On the one hand, the author of the novel, Cao Xueqin, who was addicted to drinking, had an intensive understanding of traditional Chinese wine culture. On the other hand, the fundamental aim is that the author made an effort to combine material beauty with spiritual beauty in order to deepen the theme of the work, creation of characters' imagery, exhibition of relationship of people, and development of story. "Wine" not only makes the story and character more plentiful but also intensifies the connotation and its tragedy consciousness, expands the thematic significance.

Hongloumeng is made up of 120 chapters, in 91 of which wine and wine-drinking are mentioned, including drinking parties, wine poems, songs and drinking games.

Example 24:

ST:

琼浆满返玻璃盏,玉液浓酌琥珀杯。

(《红楼梦》第五回)

TT1:

Verily, glass vessels overflowed with **nectar**
and amber cups brimmed with **ambrosia.**

(*Yang's translation*)

TT2:

Celestial nectar filled the crystal cup,
And **liquid gold** in amber goblets glowed.

(*Hawkes' translation*)

It's an outstanding poem illustrating wine, and features of Chinese wine are conveyed in virtue of "琼浆" and "玉液" which are the drinks and wines that Gods have in Greece myth. The relatively equivalent effect is achieved by the assimilation translation in Yang's version. For Hawkes, more efforts are made to achieve reader-acceptability, his rendition transfers the poet's sentiments and turns out to be more concrete and vivid on account of the two striking lines. Through the visual image of the wine, Hawkes makes something abstract concrete, so it appeals to the readers' sense of sight easily.

During the period of drinking, people often play a drinkers' game. When playing the game, one person is in charge and the others obey him to recite poems or play games in turn and will be punished if anyone violates the rules. It has been very popular since the Tang Dynasty. The drinkers must first empty their cups of wine completely before they are qualified to continue the game. It can be seen that drinkers wager game (酒令) is a form of language, and reflects the relationship between language and culture. While playing a drinker's game, the players usually quote the classics, cite allusions or wonderful sentences in literary works, which gives the language of drinkers wager game strong literary flavor. There are a great number of descriptions of these games in *Hongloumeng*, especially in Chapter Forty.

Example 25:

ST:

鸳鸯道：“凑成‘二郎游五岳’。”

薛姨妈道：“世人不及神仙乐。”

（《红楼梦》第四十回）

TT1:

“The whole: O'er **the Five Peaks the young god** wends his way.”

“Immortal joys are barred to mortal clay.”

(*Yang's translation*)

TT2:

'Together that gives: "**The Second Prince** plays in the **Five Holy Hills**".'

'The immortals dwell far off from mortal ills.'

(*Hawkes' translation*)

God Erlang is famous in China mythology. In the mythology of *the Lotus Lamp* a goddess falls in love with a mortal man and leaves for earth with her magical lotus lantern in tow. Several years later, her older brother God Erlang, is still furious at his sister's impropriety, captures her and imprisons her under Mt. Hua. God Erlang as a mythical figure is deeply rooted in Chinese culture. It's harsh for the translators to make the TT readers not only acquainted with the national characteristics of this myth, but also see the distinctive image of God Erlang. Hawkes rendered

"二郎神" into "the Second Prince", which can't be identified as a god, not to say its image or it's meaning. Besides, "the Five Holy Hills" leads to the loss of information, so does Yang's translation of "the Five Peaks". The five mountains, the collection of five holy mountains in China, are indispensable to Chinese culture, about which literary men through the ages have written poems. Although Erlang is rendered into a god in Yang's version, the readers still fail to grasp its connotation. in my opinion, neither of them succeeded in empathizing to the ST and the poet or the TT and TT readers, because Yang was unable to reserve the original cultural image or literature aesthetic value, and Hawkes was unable to come close to the TT readers.

5.4.3 Comparison of empathy in terms of social culture

In a broad sense, social culture pertains to various forms of social organizations and institutes, —how people interact and organize themselves in groups; laws, policies, virtues—how the society keeps peace; and the spiritual aspect of people—how people think about themselves and the society, and anything else, including the concept of people themselves, which exist in the society, such as folk customs, value system, kinship systems, body languages, norms of behavior, education, entertainment, sports, politics and the law, etc. Social elements play a vital role in the language and culture of a nation, and the existence and development of language are affected by society. As language is the carrier of culture, the social phenomenon and vocabulary of a certain historical periods reflect the objective history of society, which may be confusing to foreign readers. To give some examples, man in the Qing Dynasty wore a braid. In Islamic countries women are not supposed to expose their faces, so they always wear a veil. We all know that China is a country of etiquette, where the social status of the worshipped and the humble is strictly fixed. When the participants address the superiors, they apply honorifics to show respect on the one hand and make use of the self-abasing terms to depreciate their own position on the other hand. On the contrary, Western culture emphasizes the so-called "individualism", "equality" and "freedom". Thus honorifics are scarce and simple while self-abasing terms are absent from English. As for titles, Emperors in the Qing Dynasty married as many as 3000 wives who were ranked along a hierarchy of wives and concubines such as "皇后""皇贵妃""贵妃""妃""贵人""嫔", etc. The distinction among them is not easy for westerners to make. Cultural gaps exist evidently in these areas. *Hongloumeng* as an encyclopedic novel depicts a vivid picture of the cultural lives of different social classes and impresses its audience with different aspects of Chinese social culture. The following three examples will show how the true picture of social culture of the ST is rendered.

Example 26:

ST:

……幸生来,英豪阔大宽宏量,从未将儿女私情略萦心上。

好一似,霁月光风耀玉堂。

断配得才貌仙郎,博得个地久天长,准折得幼年时坎坷形状……。

（《红楼梦》第五回）

TT1:

Happily she is born too courageous and open-hearted
Ever to take a love affair to heart,
Like bright moon and fresh breeze in a hall of jade
She is matched with **a talented and handsome husband**;
May she live with him for long years
To make up for her wretched childhood!

(*Yang's translation*)

TT2:

Yet yours was a generous, open-hearted nature,
And never could be snared or soured
By childish piques and envious passions—
You were a crystal house by wind and moonlight scoured.
Matched to **a perfect, gentle husband,**
Security of bliss at last it seemed,
And all your childish miseries redeemed.

(*Hawkes' translation*)

Example 27:

ST:

凭栏人向东风泣,茜裙偷傍桃花立。

(《红楼梦》第七十回)

TT1:

Then, shedding tears alone on the balustrade;

Neath blossoming boughs slips the **red**-skirted maid.

(*Yang' translation*)

TT2:

In the soft breeze the lady's face is wet with many a tear.

Her silken **peach**-skirt billows out, the peach-trees to be near.

(*Hawkes' translation*)

Example 28:

ST:

娣探谨奉　二兄文几

(《红楼梦》第三十七回)

TT1:

Tanchun greets her **Second Brother**

(*Yang's translation*)

TT2:

Dear Brother

(*Hawkes' translation*)

In Example 26 the poem describes the destiny of Shi Xiangyun from her birth to her marriage. Values are the basic unconscious organizing principle that people abide by. Each culture has its own unique value system, which tells people what is expected by the society, what's right or wrong, what's just or unjust. Value system is a very complex area deep-rooted in the ideology of human beings. In ancient China, parents chose a suitable fiancé or fiancée for their child whose marriage was arranged by his / her parents. Even the new couple has little opportunity of seeing each other before their wedding, to say nothing of getting fond of each other. Westerners may be puzzled by such a situation—how can two strangers get married? What's more, Chinese standards for choosing a daughter/son-in-law are different from those of the West. The translation of "She is matched with a talented and handsome husband" by Yang is based on his understanding of Chinese culture; while for Western parents, they may look on a gentleman as their daughter's most ideal husband. Besides, Western parents seldom directly get involved in their children's marital problems, as long as their son or daughter is fond of his / her partner, they will agree with him / her, because they are willing to maintain intimate relationship with their children.

"茜" in Example 27 comes from the name of a red dye madder or alizarin. Hawkes used peach instead, a color that English readers would not hard to recognize; while Yang kept the name of the original.

Example 28 is a letter written by Tanchun sent to Baoyu to

invite him to take part in a poetry club. Though it is only a letter, it has generally been thought of as a poem because of its poetic language. In China, feudal society lasted for thousands of years based on a self-sufficient agricultural economy. The feudal patriarchal system has exercised a strong influence on people's psychological mind and norms. As a result, Chinese people put great emphasis on kinship and the distinction of seniority in the family. In terms of forms of address, Chinese is rich in various terms addressing teachers, master workers and family members, etc., which often causes difficulty to translators; while in English, people upholding individualism pay less attention to the order of seniority in the family or clan. It is very common for people to address each other just by the given name. *Hongloumeng* depicts the prosperity and decline of four large families, and is sure to involve the description of complicated relationships among all kinds of characters and kinfolks. In such a situation, almost all Chinese kinship terms are mentioned in this novel. Due to the above distinctive difference, how to render Chinese kinship terms is generally thought of as a demanding and challenging task. In Example 28 the difference in translation is obvious. Yang conforms to Chinese social convention and retains the Chinese cultural characteristics following rigidly the feudal ethics, whereas Hawkes replaces the Chinese elements with his own. Similarly, the ending "谨奉" has been rendered by these two translators respectively as "Respectfully written" and "Your affectionate Sister, Tanchun".

To summarize the above three examples shows that Yang aims at keeping and reflecting the Chinese characteristics, arriving at empathizing to the original and the ST author; while Hawkes places much emphasis on the receptors, arriving at empathizing to the TT and TT readers.

5.4.4 Comparison of empathy in terms of religious culture

The anthropologist Edward Burnett Tylor (1832—1917) defined religion as belief in supernatural beings and stated that this belief originated as explanations of the world. Belief in supernatural beings grew out of attempts to explain life and death. Primitive people used human dreams in which spirits seemed to appear as an indication that the human mind could exist independent of a body. They used this by extension to explain life and death, and belief in the after-life. Myths and deities to explain natural phenomena originated out of an analogy and an extension of these explanations. (Tylor, 1871) Religion, as a reflection of people's belief, is a very important component that has played a big role in every human culture. In the strict sense, it represents a kind of ethic on which society is based and survives. Thus it lies in the kernel of culture. Religious culture is such an important part of the lives of human being that it refers to the culture caused by a people's religious belief and ideology, which is expressed in taboo differences. Difference in religious culture and translation of religious culture are an important component of human culture. Confucianism, Taoism and Buddhism are three main religions in China and have immense influence on Chinese culture, whose traits are noticeably left in the Chinese language. In Chinese language, such sentences as "阿弥陀佛","菩萨保佑","跑得了和尚,跑不了庙" and "无事不登三宝殿" etc. are often heard. In contrast, in Britain, Christian culture is the mainstream of the Western culture. The Christians believe that man is born with sin and can't get rid of it by his own efforts. Most people are Christians who believe in God, because they think the world is created by God and all things in the world are arranged by God. The scripture of the Christianity has had a great impact on the English language, such as the following two well-known proverbs: the Chinese saying "谋事在人,成事在天" reflects the influence of Buddhism, and the English "Man proposes, God disposes" reflects the influence of Christianity. All in all, language and religious culture are mingled and mixed together, which influence people's ideology and thus cause some difficulty in translating. Religious beliefs are closely related to and reflected in literary works, and many expressions and sentences related to religion exist in *Hongloumeng*. The following example is typical (For full text, see Example 1.),

Example 29:

ST:

好了歌

世人都晓神仙好，惟有功名忘不了！

……

世人都晓神仙好，只有金银忘不了！

……

世人都晓神仙好，只有姣妻忘不了！

……

世人都晓神仙好，只有儿孙忘不了！

（《红楼梦》第一回）

TT1:

All Goo Things Must End

"All men long to be **immortals**,

Yet to riches and rank each aspires;

...

All men long to be **immortals**,

Yet silver and gold they prize

...

All men long to be **immortals**,

Yet dote on the wives they've wed.

...

All men long to be **immortals**,

Yet with getting sons won't have done.

(*Yang's translation*)

TT2:

Won-Done Song

Men all know that **salvation** should be won,
But with ambition won't have done, have done.
...
Men all know that **salvation** should be won,
But with their riches won't have done, have done.
...
Men all know that **salvation** should be won,
But with their loving wives they won't have done.
...
Men all know that **salvation** should be won,
But with their children won't have done, have done.
...

(*Hawkes' version*)

In Taoism "神仙" is a basic concept which refers to an immortal, a person who has the power of clairvoyance or complete freedom from worldly troubles. To become "神" or "仙" is the highest ideal of Taosim. So this sentence can be paraphrased like this, "All men know that it is good to be an immortal and all want to become immortals". Yang took a direct approach and rendered it into "immortal". In contrast, the concept of salvation is typical in Christianity in the West where human beings are born with "original sin", so they have to pray all their life for salvation. Therefore, Hawkes replaced the concept with his own religious concept of "salvation", and translated the sentence as "Men all know that salvation should be won". Thus, Hawkes produces a totally different religious concept which is likely to mislead the foreign readers who would think that Chinese people have the same religious belief as theirs although it offers a more acceptable version to the TT readers and empathizes to them.

5.4.5 Comparison of empathy in terms of linguistic culture

There are numerous kinds of languages in the world, and each language carries its own characteristics besides the marvelous differences in the number of users, the area of spread and its influence. Meanwhile, language, as discussed before, is the carrier of culture and in turn, it reflects culture. Linguistic culture refers to the specific characteristics of the related language. "Translation problems can also arise from structural differences in the vocabulary, syntax and supersegmental feature of the two languages." (Nord, 2001: 66)

Example 30:

ST:

富贵不知乐业，贫困难耐凄凉。
可怜辜负好时光，于国于家无望。

（《红楼梦》第三回）

TT1:

Left cold by **riches and nobility,**
Unfit to bear the stings of poverty,
He wastes his time and his ability,
Failing his **country and his family.**

(*Yang's translation*)

TT2:

Prosperous, he could not play his part with **grace,**
Nor, poor, bear hardship with a smiling face.
So shamefully the precious hours he'd waste
That both **indoors and out** he was disgraced.

(*Hawkes' translation*)

Example 31:

ST:

衰草枯杨,曾为歌舞场。

(《红楼梦》第一回)

TT1:

Dead weeds and **withered trees,**
Where men have once **danced and sung.**

(*Yang's translation*)

TT2:

Bleak haunts where weeds and willows scarcely thrive,
Were once with **mirth and revelry** alive.

(*Hawkes' translation*)

Example 30 includes "富""贵""贫""困""国"and"家", each of which bears an independent meaning in ancient Chinese. Yang, as a Chinese literati, is well-versed in ancient Chinese, and has no trouble understanding that in Cao Xueqin's times, these two characters indicated two separate notions. Being empathetic to the original author, he translated "富贵" into "riches and nobility", "国"and"家"into "country" and "family". Compared with Yang's, these Chinese characters were combined into one unit in Hawkes', which were made more easily accepted and understood by Western readers.

"衰草" and "枯杨" in Example 31 are directly rendered into "dead weeds" and "withered trees" in Yang's translation. Hawkes adds "bleak haunts" to create wild scenery by changing the original parallel nominal phrase into an attributive clause that is a typical syntax of English.

Since ancient times, Chinese people have been expressing and celebrating their joy by singing and dancing. In the Chinese language, some expressions and phrases have been generated to describe the scene of great joy and prosperity, such as "载歌载舞" (festively singing and dancing), "莺歌燕舞" (orioles sing and swallows dart-a scene of prosperity), and "歌舞升平" (sing and dance to extol the good times-put on a false show of peace and prosperity) etc. Therefore, "歌舞" (sing and dance) are almost kept intact in Yang's version, which tries to remain within the original culture. By empathizing to the original, not only the form of language is reproduced but also the "force" or the meaning of the original; while in Hawkes' version, "歌舞" is revised into the term of "mirth and revelry" that carries an abstract image—a boisterous and perhaps, alcohol-involved merrymaking scene. As a result it seems familiar to the English readers. Though the concrete actions (dance and sing) are absent, it is successful in empathizing to the TT readers.

Like other literary works, *Hongloumeng* is imbued with many rhetoric devices, such as metaphors, similes, allusions, puns, personification and so on, where a lot of cultural elements are embedded.

Example 32:

ST:

珍珠如土金如铁。

(《红楼梦》第四回)

TT1:

Gold is **like** iron to them
And pearls like sand.

(*Yang's translation*)

TT2:

To count their money
Would take all day...

(*Hawkes' translation*)

Yang's version keeps close to the original in both form and sense by rendering "如" correspondently into "like" in English and he translates the simile to simile arriving at empathizing to the ST. While in the latter, the symbol of wealth—“珍珠”, “金” is deserted, and large amount of “土”, “铁” implied is absent, too; at the same time, it is deprived of the vivid picture depicting Xue's affluence. But if we look at the poem as a whole, we will see that the translation of Hawkes is more rhythmical, more vivacious and poem-like, less rigid in style, and the beauty in sound is created.

Metaphor as a rhetorical device is popular in both the Chinese and English languages. As a higher form of description, illustration and illumination, it requires greater ability on the part of the readers to perceive the implication, the insight into persons, things or ideas hidden in it.

Example 33:

ST:

应惭西子，实愧王嫱。

（《红楼梦》第五回）

TT1:

She would put his **Shih** to shame to make **Wang Chiang** blush.

(*Yang's translation*)

TT2:

The beauties of the days gone by her beauty are all abashed.

(*Hawkes' translation*)

Example 34:

ST:

出浴太真冰作影子,捧心西子玉为魂。

(《红楼梦》第三十七回)

TT1:

Like Lady Yang's shade, fresh from the bath, ice-pure,
Or his Shih's mournful spirit fair as jade.

(*Yang's translation*)

TT2:

A Yang-fei risking naked from the bath,
With a cool, chast allure that she had not.

(*Hawkes' translation*)

Metaphors are abundant in Chinese culture. When translating them, translators can make some shifts to deal with them including not only their meanings but also the peculiar cultures according to the concrete condition. In the above poems, crab apple flower (白海棠) is compared to the well-known beauty Yang Yuhuan and Xi Shi by the author. Xi Shi was one of the Four Renowned Beauties of ancient China, who was said to have lived during the end of the Spring and Autumn Dynasty. So was Yang Yuhuan during the Tang Dynasty. And Wang Qiang was a beauty of the Han Dynasty. All of them are household beauties and now have become the substitutes of beauty. Thus it sounds familiar to the Chinese, but it's hard for the English readers to imagine and appreciate such beauty. So in Example 33 Hawkes changes the metaphor into plain narrative expressions taking only a universal expression "beauty" instead, leaving out the images of Xi Shi and Wang Qiang. Also, as golden and suntan skin is beautiful and healthy according to western standards, they may fail to understand in what way fair and smooth skin is beautiful, but it's easy for Chinese readers to appreciate such beautiful skin "fair as jade", So Hawkes omits the metaphor in Example 34 by empathizing towards the TT readers.

Chapter Six
Comparison of Pragmatic Empathy in Poetry Translation in *Hongloumeng*

6.1 Theory of pragmatic empathy

In 1991, Professor He Ziran published an article entitled "Pragmatic empathy in linguistic communication", in which he put forward his idea of the application of empathy to linguistic communication in detail, and made a systematic study of pragmatic empathy as a communicative strategy. He holds that, "In pragmatics, the participants of one conversation try to imagine, understand and share their conversational partners' intentions and feelings through role-taking. So, in the conversational communication, the speaker deliberately uses languages to express his beliefs, intentions, ideas, etc. from the perspective of his hearer so as to make his utterance quite acceptable for the hearer; while the hearer tries to understand the meaning of the utterance by taking the speaker's perspective." He divided pragmatic empathy into two types: pragma-linguistic empathy and socio-pragmatic empathy. (何自然, 1991: 11. The translation is mine.)

6.1.1 Pragma-linguistic empathy

Pragma-linguistic empathy refers to the fact that the speaker deliberately uses language to express his attitudes and intentions; and the hearer understands the speaker's intentions form the viewpoint of the speaker. In Professor He's opinion, the following example can well illustrate what it means:

e.g. What a bit of luck that I'm placed next to you.

In this example, the addressor can step into the addressee's shoes, which has made the utterances polite and pleasant to the addressee. Thus, this utterance is more that appropriate. On the contrary, if the addressor had not used empathy, the consequence would have been quite different. If he had said: "What a bit of luck that you are placed next to me", the communicative effect would be different. It's obvious that this utterance might not sound comfortable to the addressee, and might even make the addressee annoyed. Thus, the pragmatic effects of these two utterances are totally different.

6.1.2 Socio-pragmatic empathy

Socio-pragmatic empathy refers to the fact that the addressor and the addressee may take the other's point and respect his ideas, custom, thinking, religions, and values, thus reaching tacit understanding in language to achieve the expected goals. When we are dealing with inter-cultural communication, we are often confronted with languages, rules and norms different from our own. In a word, empathy in socio-pragmatics focuses on the social, cultural backgrounds of the communicators and communicative context. Therefore, it is important for us to be fully aware of not only our own culture but also that of others. For example, people whose native language is Chinese should respect the pragmatic habits of people from other cultures.

The following example shows that different cultural thinking leads to misunderstanding in inter-cultural communication. A is a Chinese student who studies in the U. S. A, and B is a local resident.

A: You look pale, what's the matter?

B: I'm feeling sick. A cold, maybe.

A: Go and see the doctor. Drink more water. Did you take any pills? Chinese medicine works wonderful. Would you like to try? Put on more clothes. Have a good rest.

B: You are not my mother, are you? (quoted in 刘心爽, 2009: 9)

In this conversation, it seems that A is ready to help others and gives some advice to B when B is in trouble. It is sure that A is popular among Chinese. However, B comes from the U. S. A, where people are oriented with individualism and value independence. On the contrary, Chinese value collectivism. So B is offended by the utterance of A. A should have taken the socio-pragmatic aspect of empathy into consideration to avoid this in order to communicate with others successfully and smoothly. This kind of pragmatic empathy is a general phenomenon of "when in Rome, do as the Romes do", and it requires that both the addressor and addressee should respect each other's thinking and views and respond appropriately.

6.2 Comparison of pragmatic empathy

According to the viewpoint of socio-pragmatic empathy, in order to communicate successfully, the addressee and addresser are supposed to respect each other's thoughts, views and feelings. From the angle of communication, literary translation from Chinese to English is also a kind of inter-cultural communication which reproduces the Chinese cultural forms taking Chinese culture as its background by English expressions. A translator as one party of communication requires psychological empathy to be successful in communication. In the translation of poetry of *Hongloumeng*, Yang has a good command of Chinese cultural images, which leads to his psychological empathy towards the ST and the ST author by reserving the original cultural color. At the same time, TT readers as the other party of communication know that they themselves are reading a translated version that talks about foreign events and foreigners, so that they respect the exotic situation and culture and transfer feeling into the version by putting themselves into others' place. On the contrary, when translating the poetry in *Hongloumeng*, Hawkes empathizes towards the TT and TT readers and tries every means to pave the way for TT readers to read and appreciate the versions, taking into consideration the acceptability of the text for TT readers. Then a few examples will be cited to illustrate the differences from the perspective of pragmatic empathy.

Example 35:

ST:

绿蓑江上秋闻笛,红袖楼头夜倚栏。

(《红楼梦》第四十八回)

TT1:

In green coir cape on the river he listens to autumn fluting,
In red sleeves she leans **over her balustrade at night**.

(*Yang's translation*)

TT2:

Where, by **a fisherman**'s sad **flute** entranced,
A lady leans out from her **casement** high.

(*Hawkes' translation*)

The above poem is rich in cultural images. Some images such as "绿蓑", "秋闻笛", "红袖", "夜倚栏", etc. are all well reproduced in Yang's version— "in green coir cape", "autumn fluting", "in red sleeves" and "over her balustrade at night". "倚栏" is aptly expressed by the expression "over her balustrade", because the word "balustrade" conveyed almost all the emotional rhyme and Chinese cultural connotation as fully as that in the original, such as Chinese architectural characteristics and Chinese idle and quiet living habit etc. However, Hawkes' translation is greatly different from Yang's, "绿蓑" and "秋闻笛" are understood as "a fisherman is playing the flute", and "红袖" as "lady", who looked out of the high window when she heard the flute melody. What's more, "casement" (阁楼上的窗口) that reflects western cultural characteristics in Hawkes' version is corresponding to "balustrade" in Yang's. The reason why the images of "绿蓑", "秋闻笛", "红袖", "夜倚栏", etc. are weakened or even omitted by Hawkes is that he intends to empathize to the readers in order to relieve the stress of English readers in reading comprehension. On the contrary, Yang makes special efforts to render these images so as to keep the cultural images and literature aesthetic value for the purpose of empathizing to the ST author and SL.

Example 36:

ST:

枉凝眉

一个是<u>**阆苑仙葩**</u>，一个是美玉无瑕。若说没<u>**奇缘**</u>，<u>**今生**</u>偏又遇着他，若说有奇缘，如何心事终虚化？一个枉自嗟呀，一个空劳牵挂。一个是水中月，一个是镜中花。想眼中能有多少泪珠儿，怎经得秋流到冬尽，春流到夏！（《红楼梦》第五回）

TT1:

Vain Longing

One is an **immortal** flower of **fairyland**,
The other fair flawless jade,
And were it not **predestined**
Why should they meet again in this **existence**?
Yet, if predestined,
Why does their love come to nothing?
One sighs to no purpose,
The other yearns in vain;
One is the moon reflected in the water,
The other but a flower in the mirror.
How many tears can well from her eyes?
Can they flow on from autumn till winter,
From spring till summer?

(*Yang's translation*)

TT2:

Hope Betrayed

One was a flower from **paradise**,
One a pure jade without spot or stain.
If each for the other one was not **intended**,
Then why **in this life** did they meet again?
And yet if fate bad meant them for each other,
Why was their earthly meeting all in vain?
In vain were all her sighs and tears,
In vain were all his anxious fears:

All, insubstantial, doomed to pass,
As moonlight mirrored in the water
Or flowers reflected in a glass.
Row many tears from those poor eyes could flow,
Which every season rained upon her woe?

(*Hawkes' translation*)

By contrast, Yang's version is more likely to demonstrate the Chinese cultural atmosphere with profound connotation; and Hawkes' seems easier to understand and more clear. It is because the two translators empathize to different targets purposefully. "阆苑仙葩", "奇缘" and "今生" in the original are concepts in Taoist and Buddhist culture, all of which bring readers who are familiar with Chinese culture special imagination. Yang uses "immortal", "fairyland", "predestined" and "existence" to convey those concepts, which has the same effect as the original one. The sentence "怎经得秋流到冬尽，春流到夏" is regarded as a hint in the novel, which means that Daiyu shed tears in sorrow and died in summer. It's obvious that Yang tried to obey the original intention and rendered it into "Can they flow on from autumn till winter, from spring till summer?". But the above-mentioned aspects are weakened in Hawkes' and they were rendered into "paradise", "intended", "in this life" and "how many tears form those poor eyes could flow, which every season rained upon her woe?" respectively, which undoubtedly caters to the reading expectation psychology of common readers.

Chapter Seven
Possible Explanations for Two Empathetic Approaches: Empathy to ST and the Author v.s. Empathy to TT and Readers

It is universally accepted that human beings have similar physiological structure and share a lot in both physical and mental activities. Therefore, anything expressed in one language can also be expressed in another language with reasonable accuracy by establishing equivalent points of reference in the receptor's culture and matching his cognitive framework by restructuring the constitutive elements of the message, and all texts are translatable. The translated versions of *Hongloumeng* also serve as good examples for translatability. But similarities between two different languages do not prevent us from seeing the differences behind them. Based on the contrastive analysis of the poetry translation of the two translated versions of *Hongloumeng* from the perspective of empathy, we can perceive a general principle governing Yang's and Hawkes' translation—Yang adhered more to the ST, empathized towards the ST and the author and tried to introduce Chinese culture to western readers as much as possible, while on the contrary Hawkes was much more reader-oriented, empathizing towards the TT and the readers in order to please the readers of TT. In this chapter, possible explanations will be put forward.

7.1 Theoretic explanations of empathy

Fortunately, great breakthroughs of translation theories have been put forward in translation studies and provided substantial support for translation studies. Firstly, skopos theory convinces us of the translator's difference in gaining his translating purpose. Secondly, Hermeneutics, a theory of philosophy about understanding or interpreting the meaning of a text, is applied to justify the display of translators' difference in the understanding and expressing stages in translating activity. Thirdly, Deconstruction concept declares that translators are subjects of creation.

7.1.1 Skopos theory

Skopos is the Greek word for "aim" or "purpose" and was introduced into translation theory in the 1970s by Hans J. Vermeer as a technical term for the purpose of a translation and of action of translating. He defines human action as intentional, purposeful behaviour that takes place in a given situation and translation is a type of human action. Therefore, translation is purposeful. Skopos theory stresses the interactional, pragmatic aspects of translation, arguing that the shape of TT should above all be determined by the function or "skopos" that it is intended to fulfill in the target context. According to skopos theory, the prime principle determining any translation process is the purpose of the overall translation action. Reiss and Vermeer specify this principle in two skopos rules: "an interaction is determined by its purpose", and "skopos can be said to vary according to the recipient." (Reiss and Vermeer, quoted in Munday) These two rules allow the translator to use the translation strategies which are most appropriate for achieving the purpose for which TT is intended, irrespective of whether they are considered to be the "standard" way to proceed in a particular translation context. That is to say, the top-ranking rule for any translation is "the end justifies the means." (Reiss and Vermeer, 1984: 101) Vermeer views translation as a type of transfer where communicative verbal and non-verbal signs are transferred from one language into another. He also considers translation as a kind of human action, an intentional, purposeful behaviour that takes place in a given situation; it is part of the situation at the same time as it modifies the situation. (Nord, 2001: 11)

Since translation is a purposeful action, every translator must possess a certain "Skopos" when translating, and each of his translation works may serve a given purpose. Thus, as the operator of the translation activity, the translator is confronted with all kinds of choices: what to translate, for whom and for what purpose to translate, and how to translate. The decision-making process leaves large room for the translator to exercise his subjectivity. As for the skopos theory, Vermeer explains,

"Each text is produced for a given purpose and should serve the purpose. The skopos rule thus reads as follows, "translate / interpret / speak / write in a way that enables your text/ translation to function in the situation in which it is used and with the people who want to use it and precisely in the way they want it to function." (Vermeer, 1989a: 20)

According to this theory, the intended target-text receiver, also referred to as the addressee of the translation, is a decisive factor in determining the production of the target text. One of the most important factors that determine the purpose of a translation is the addressee, who is the intended receiver or audience of the target text with their culture-specific world knowledge, their expectations and their communicative needs. Every translation should be directed at an intended addressee, because to translate means "to produce a target text setting for a target purpose and target addressees in target circumstances." (Vermeer, 1987: 29, quoted in Nord, 2001: 12) The translation norms have moved from faithfulness or equivalence to the concern with the target language texts acceptability. In translating, each translator has his own readers. They might be himself, his friends or anyone in the receptor world. Before translating, he should have a very clear picture of the needs of the readers, so translation is a process with a clear objective, by which the translator always determines his methods and strategies. Thus, one advantage of skopos theory is that it allows the possibility of the same text being translated in different ways according to the purpose of the TT and the commission given to the translator. In Vermeer's words:

What the skopos states is that one must translate, consciously and consistently, in accordance with some principle respecting the target text. The theory does not state what the principle is: this must be decided separately in each specific case. (quoted in Munday, 2001: 80)

The two different empathetic approaches may be explained from Yang's and Hawkes' translation briefs and skopos. According to the skopos theory, in translational action, it is the initiator and commissioner that produce the translation brief. In Yang's translational process, the commissioner is the publishing house—Foreign Language Press where Yang and Gladys Yang worked. Therefore, some restraints were imposed on them, especially against the background with a heavy political atmosphere (The great Cultural Revolution influence). Different from Yang, Hawkes was much luckier to enjoy more freedom in choosing the works to translate. He signed a contract with Penguin Books in 1970. Thus, both the publishing press and Hawkes are the formulations of the translation brief, which directly influences the translation methods and strategies employed in the whole process. On the other hand, differences also lie in the addressee and receiver. The addressees of Yang's version are some foreigners or experts who are interested in Chinese culture and have certain knowledge about it.

Hawkes always takes the target readers into consideration while translating. In the translation, he bridged up the gaps between two totally different cultures and languages in order to make it easy for his readers to understand. He says in his preface to *The Story of the Stone*:

"My one abiding principle has been to translate everything —even puns. For although this is, in the sense I have already indicated, an "unfinished" novel, it was written (and rewritten) by a great artist with is very lifeblood. I have therefore assumed that whatever I find in it is therefore a purpose and must be dealt with somehow or other. I cannot pretend always to have done so successfully, but if I can convey to the reader even a fraction of the pleasure this Chinese novel given to me, I shall not have lived in vain." (Hawkes, 1973)

In the preface of it, we can obviously observe that he translated *Hongloumeng* mainly out of his admiration for the novel, and he had a strong motive to share with the readers the enthusiasm and passion he felt towards this great novel as well as the delight he got from it. His translation is basically empathetic to the readers and TT.

These words give a general idea about Hawkes' translation skopos. As he is so much interested in the great novel, he gives a complete translated text of it in order to actualize his long cherished dream. What's more, he intends to bring the profound Chinese culture and the masterpiece to English readers. Therefore, his skopos requires him to adopt the approach of empathy to the readers and TT.

For Yang's part, there is no translator's introduction or postscript in his version, so readers don't know his translation purpose or attitude. Instead in a symposium held in Austria in March 1980, Yang Xianyi said that the Chinese people should know more about the foreign heritage and the foreign people also should know about Chinese cultural heritage. He claimed, "I don't think it proper to interpret excessively in translation, so a translator should try his best to be loyal to the images of the original. Of course, if something equivalent can't be found in translation, some meanings of the original have to be sacrificed. Too much importance attached to the creativity is wrong, otherwise, it would not be translation but adaptation. A translator should be loyal to the core of Chinese culture, to the spirit of Chinese civilization. This is not only an issue concerned with the translation of Chinese cultural heritage, but also with how to convey the value and spirit of Chinese culture, convey Chinese people's everyday life, their happiness and sorrow, their love and hatred, their pity and bitterness, as well as their fondness and anger." (qtd. 任生名, 1993: 33. The translation is mine.)

The above-mentioned ideas clearly indicate that Yang tries

to convey the Chinese culture as faithfully as he can to the English-speaking countries for the purpose of spreading Chinese culture. Since the skopos is what a translator should stick to in his translation, therefore, the skopos of Yang's translation calls for the approach of empathy to the author and ST.

It is known that different translation briefs will cause different translated versions. This is true of *A Dream of Red Mansions* and *The Story of the Stone*. Since translation is a purposeful action, every translator must possess a certain "skopos" when translating, and each of his translated works may serve a given purpose. Yang's and Hawkes' versions are presented in the diagram below for comparison.

Table 7.1 The comparison of Yang's version and Hawkes' version

Translation Brief	**Yang's version**	**Hawkes' version**
The (intended) text function(s)	Spread the excellent Chinese culture and language to western countries	Bring the pleasure of reading this great novel to westerners
Commissioner and initiator	The publishing house-Foreign Language Press	David Hawkes and publishing house-Penguin Books
The target-text addressee(s)	Western readers who are interested in Chinese culture and want to know more; Chinese readers who major in English, Hongloumeng and Redologists	Western readers who are interested in Chinese culture and read for entertainment

Continued Table

Translation Brief	Yang's version	Hawkes' version
The (prospective) time of text reception	Around the late of 1970s	the same
The (prospective) place of text reception	English-speaking countries and China	English-speaking countries
The medium over which the text will be transmitted	Books	Books
The motive for the production of the text	Introduce the great Chinese classic to western readers	Realize his long-cherished dream and recommend a masterpiece to western readers
The motive for the reception of the text	Get further understanding of Chinese and its culture; learn Chinese-English translation	Read for entertainment

According to their different translation briefs and skopos, Yang mainly empathizes to the author and the ST, and Hawkes to the western readers and the TT. Let's look at two more examples, and we can have a better idea how Yang and Hawkes meet the requirements of their translation briefs.

Example 37:

ST:

松影一庭惟见鹤,梨花满地不闻莺。

(《红楼梦》第十二回)

TT1:

Only a stork can be seen in the pine-shadowed court.

No oriole sings in the snow which has drifted like pear-blossom.

(*Yang's translation*)

TT2:

Only a stork outside is to be found.

No orioles mow, though white flowers mask the ground.

(*Hawkes' translation*)

In China, some of the plants and flowers have specific connotations, which can arouse a great deal of imagination. As is known to all, in ancient Chinese poetry, image is often used to transmit the artistic conception. For example, the Chinese word "松" is usually taken as the symbol of one's tenacity, purity and longevity and the word "兰" as the symbol of one's moral integrity, virtue and temperament. In this poem, "松" and "鹤" are used together in order to present a peaceful and harmonious image in readers' minds even though there is no "松" or "鹤" in the real situation. Moreover, the writer compared "snow" to "梨花" (pear-blossom), which may be familiar to Chinese readers. However, it is not easy for some Western readers to apprehend such an image connotation.

It can be seen from the above diagram that Yang's translation skopos is to introduce the Chinese culture to

Westerners. Therefore, he translates "松影一庭" and "鹤" into "the pine-shadowed court" and "a stork" directly. By translating "梨花" into "the snow which has drifted like pear-blossom", he shows the metaphorical meaning of "梨花" clearly and the Westerners become informed of one often-used metaphor in Chinese poetry. He transmits not only the linguistic form but also the cultural content.

Hawkes' translation skopos is to bring the readers enjoyment through reading. Therefore, the metaphor is avoided purposefully, which he thinks is strange to his readers. In his translation, he has only preserved "鹤" and abandoned "松" for the sake of the rhythm and alleviating the burden of his readers to get the connotation of the metaphor and replaces the Chinese metaphor with an English expression by translating "梨花" into "white flowers" which is ready to be accepted and understood by English readers.

Example 38:

ST:

杜蔼桐阴坐举觞,长安涎口盼重阳。

（《红楼梦》第三十八回）

TT1:

We sit, cups raised, in the shade of osmanthus and Wu-tong;
Mouths watering, for **<u>the Double Ninth</u>** we pine;

(*Yang's translation*)

TT2:

With wine cups in hand, as **<u>the autumn day</u>** ends,

And with watering mouths, we await our small friends.

(*Hawkes' translation*)

Chong Yang Festival is one of the traditional festivals in China celebrated on the ninth day of the ninth lunar month, and it is also called the Double Ninth Festival. In an ancient and mysterious book *Yi Jing*, or *The Book of Changes*《易经》, number "6" was thought to be of *Yin* character, meaning feminine or negative, while number "9" was thought to be *Yang*, meaning masculine or positive. So the number nine in both month and day creates the Double Ninth Festival, or Chongyang Festival. *Chong* in Chinese means "double". Also, as double ninth was pronounced the same as the word to signify "forever", the ancient Chinese considered it an auspicious day worth celebrating. That's why ancient Chinese began to celebrate this festival long time ago. It is also known as "Respect-for-the-Aged-Day", when people show deep respect for the aged by visiting them with gifts and wishing them health and longevity. Climbing mountains, carrying a spray of dogwood believed to drive away evil spirits and drinking chrysanthemum wine are also the traditional activities on this day.

In Yang's version, "重阳" is translated as "the Double Ninth". The peculiarity of the ST is fully embodied in the TT through the document translation, which serves Yang's translation briefs of introducing Chinese culture. Since "the Double Ninth" doesn't exist in English culture, Hawkes uses a single word "autumn" instead in his version. Probably, he thinks that there is no urge or necessity to introduce the China-specific festival to burden the English readers in their reading. From the word "autumn", the readers can only infer the time when the festival falls. It is easy to see that Hawkes chooses to empathize to his readers by mainly conforming to the TT culture.

7.1.2 Hermeneutics

Hermeneutics, in a broad sense, a theory of philosophy about understanding the meaning of a text, has undergone several stages: hermeneutics in Ancient Greece, hermeneutics in the middle age, methodological hermeneutics, ontological hermeneutics, and philosophical hermeneutics. Martin Heidegger (1889—1976) and Hans-Georg Gadamer (1900—2002) are the important contemporary representatives. Heidegger proposes that understanding itself is the existing mode of being and the original understanding is a "fore-understanding", which constitutes the "angle of view" for being's existence, (Heidegger, 1999: 191) and Gadamer, as one of his students, inherits Heidegger's theory and develops it into a more systematic modern philosophical hermeneutics. And it is Gadamer who uses literary criticism in a new phase of insisting on the importance of readers and brings about the boom of reader-oriented theories. He argues that the historical and temporal situation of an interpreter can never be excluded from hermeneutics, and the role of translator as a reader is not a passive recipient of meaning but an active and creative agent in the making of meaning. He also sticks to his view that a literary text is not a finished self-sustained unit of meaning. No interpretation can be final. Understanding is a dynamic process between the interpreters and the text. Hence an inescapable relativity and indeterminacy are introduced into the process of interpretation, in this process, the translation inevitably carries the translator's own subjective color, which leads to different versions of the same ST. It is George Steiner who combines philosophical hermeneutics with translation studies and forms a systematic hermeneutic translation theory. He points out that "as much research into the reading process has shown, each act of reading a text is in itself an act of translation, i. e. an interpretation. Inevitably, we feed our own beliefs, knowledge, attitudes and so on into our processing of texts, so that any translation will, to some extent, reflect the translator's own mental and cultural outlook." (Hatim and Mason, 2001: 10–11)

As a theory exploring the comprehension and interpretation of meaning, it provides a theoretical perspective which is effective for translation researches, especially the basic notions of philosophical hermeneutics— "fore-understanding", "prejudice" and "fusion of horizons". Fore-understanding is proposed by

Heidegger. According to him, any understanding or interpretation is dependent on the interpreter's pre-understanding, and it is precisely our being-in-the-world with its presuppositions and prejudices that makes understanding possible and feasible. In fact, fore-understanding is a kind of cognitive structure of an interpreter, which submerges in the process of comprehension. Gadamer put forward "prejudice" on the basis of "fore-understanding" initiated by Heidegger. "Prejudice" refers to the judgement and orientation of an interpreter formed under a certain historical condition. Every one is embedded in a certain historical situation and possesses prejudice. Gadamer says that "understanding is an event that we are involved in, but we cannot determine it. We never enter the world of cognition with nothing in hand, but instead always face it with familiar beliefs and expectations. The understanding comprises not only the strange world that we encounter suddenly, but also the familiar one that we own. " (quoted in谢天振, 2000: 54. The translation is mine.) He (1975: 245) also claims that prejudice is not an obstacle but the basis for the possibility of understanding since it serves as the interpreter's orientation to meaning. Seen in this light, "fore-understanding" and "prejudice" offer insight into the role played by the translators and lay emphasis on the translators' creative labor, subjective color and unique style. The components of prejudice in literary reading are regarded as those including language, experience, memories, motives, intentions, emotions and sub-consciousness. “Understanding is not a process of duplication but of creation. It is safe to say that as long as man is the doer of understanding there exist different interpretations.” (Gadamer, 1976: 218) In this sense, when different translators are ready to translate the same literary works, they possess different fore-understanding structures and prejudices, with which they start communicating with the ST and the author from their own perception and end up in a diversity of versions. Inevitably they will fill in the gaps and indeterminacies in the translated text in accordance with their aesthetic experience, cultural consciousness and bilingual competence. With individual specificity, different translators may adhere to different translation standards and employ different translation approaches. In the case of poetry translation in *Hongloumeng*, Yang mainly utilizes the approach of empathy to the ST and the author in translation with the prejudice to preserve the cultural identity and bring to mind exotic images and mystery. Hawkes adopts the approach of empathy to the TT and the readers with the prejudice for the westerners to enjoy through reading.

“Fusion of horizons” is another central concept advanced by Gadamer. Horizon refers to every person’s and every text’s pre-determinacy and openness brought about by “fore-understanding” and “prejudice”. He argues that different historical situations lead to different horizons, and different individuals own different horizons, which are not closed but open. Due to the change of circumstances and the distance of time between the author and the reader, there are distances and differences between the two horizons. All interpretation of past literature arises from a dialogue between past and present. Understanding is a process of fusing of the text's and interpreter's horizons. In translation, translators communicate with the ST and fuse their present horizons with their past horizons, and even give rise to a whole new horizon which not only embodies but also surpasses the original horizons of the author and the reader, only to form diverse new horizons or different interpreted versions. No matter how hard the translator may have tried to empathize with the author, it cannot be simply a re-awakening of the original event in the mind of the writer. Rather, it is a recreation of a text that is guided by how the translator understands what is said in it.

In the light of hermeneutic ideas, different translators, with varied pre-structured knowledge or "fore-understanding" or "prejudice", set out their translation practice, ending up in their individualistic interpretation of a single ST. Hermeneutics can account for the fact that different translators will show great diversity in their interpretation of the same original due to their different or changing horizons.

7.1.3 Deconstruction view

Deconstruction theory originated in the mid-1960s in France, with Derrida, Foucault and Venuti as its representatives, who introduced it into translation studies, stating that translators are subjects of creation, and translated versions are created new-born language. From the perspective of deconstruction, translation is a process of continuously revising or delaying the source text in order to replace the ST. It is a regulated transformation from one language to another and one text to another. For Derrida, the term "regulated transformation" can reflect the characteristics of translation much better than the word "translation". The status of a translator is raised, which greatly justify the translator's own subjectivity and creativity. The artistic value of the text should not be placed higher than the target text. The relationship between the ST and the TT is symbiotic but not derivative, and they complement and restrict each other. The translator will interpret and translate the ST creatively according to his own knowledge background, social experiences and cultural awareness and so on. Therefore, different translated versions by different translators are inevitable to the same ST either in language or in the styles. Every translated version is the différance and substitution of the ST. Deconstructionists hold the view that there is difference between signifier and signified and language is the play of differences from the signifier to the signified. The meaning of the original text is uncertain; it even proceeds with an endless process of signs differing to other signs, which advocates that there exists no fixed meaning of the original text and once it is finished, the original author dies in a certain sense since the text has its own life and the author has no right to say anything about the translated version, since the translator who is endowed with more freedom and rights comes into being. Translation not only can be understood according to the translator's understanding, but also can be written. The meaning develops only as the reader interacts with the text, the social and cultural elements. Therefore, it is the translator's choice to interpret the text, to get what the text contains according to his understanding.

7.2 Features of Chinese poetic language that allow for expansion

Literature is the art of language, and in a sense, language itself is an art. Sapir in *Language*: *An Introduction to the Study of Speech* set a high value on language, "Language is the most vast and profound art that we have ever known, and as great as mountains." (quoted in 陆卓元, 1985: 197. The translation is mine.) The art of language enriches literature, especially the endless poetic taste. Chinese character as a special language form has its own characteristics, such as the form of Chinese character and taste, melody and rhetoric and so on. In the meantime, the uniqueness of Chinese is helpful to the development and flourish of a lyrical style, especially poetry. Chinese poetry features also allow for expansion on the basis of readers' understanding.

7.2.1 Vividness

Poetic language originates from daily spoken language, though it is above spoken language. Poetic language is "image language displaying literary aesthetic significance by vivid perceptual appearance and rich rational connotations, which is characterized by arousing our aesthetic intuition, expanding semantics continuously, and finally increasing the distance with non-literary language by synchronic concretization and polysemy." (董学文、张永刚, 2001: 35. The translation is mine.) Seen in this light, poetic language has the features of concretization in speech form (语表) combined with polysemy in speech sense (语里). Language concretization refers to the fact that literary language stimulates sensory organs and arouses the readers' imagination of some concrete objects, and polysemy in speech sense means various meanings which are difficult for abstract thinking to generalize hidden meaning in concretization in speech form. These two features depend on each other and perfectly complement each other. The sentence "空篱旧圃秋无痕，冷月清霜梦有知" in the poem of *thinking of the chrysanthemum* implies that the bare fence and old flower bed make people realize spring has gone with the chrysanthemum;

the moon in the sky and the frost on the ground may strike the thoughts and feelings and make us see chrysanthemum again in dream. The images of "空篱" "旧圃" "冷月" and "清霜" form a desolate picture that make us disconsolate and sad. What one recalls is a gardenful of beautiful autumn tints, cheerful fellow travelers, the sweetheart, or the fleeting time besides the chrysanthemum. Readers have different association for concrete images, without which the appeal and aesthetic value of the poem will be lost. Thus, to a certain extent, images and semantic meaning are inseparable. But from the angle of translation, sense and form of literary language, namely, the form and contents are driven apart in most cases. Basically, when one language is translated into another language, the language form has changed with only the form interpreted, which detaches the sense form from the sense. In this case, sense is likely to differ from person to person.

Writing poems requires image thinking. Poetry is the expression of thoughts, which awakes higher and nobler emotions or their opposites. It is the song of man's heart and soul, the picture of man's senses and imaginations. Poetic language should be more concrete, vivid and imagic. Poetic image is the essential factor and soul of poetry. Language tends to be the carrier of the poetic image. Actually, the process of creating a poem is a kind of process in which the poet will select suitable concrete objects to be the poetic images, and construct the poetic image language so as to express his subjective feelings vividly. To achieve and strengthen its vividness and artistry, abundant figures of speech are commonly employed. Chinese is an ideographic writing as well as pictograph, and its imagic nature contributes to image thinking; while western language is just a single "phonetics center" lacking sensibility and image, which is very different from Chinese character. Thus, Chinese is likely to contain more images and is more imagic.

Example 39:

ST:

西江月

汉苑零星有限，隋堤点缀无穷。

三春事业付东风，明月梅花一梦。

……

（《红楼梦》第七十回）

TT1:

Few and far between in the Han Garden,

They make the whole Sui Dyke gleam!

Their spring splendour gone with the wind,

Moonlight and plum-blossom nothing but a dream.

...

(*Yang's translation*)

TT2:

In the Han palace garden a scatter thin and slight,

But along the Sui embankment in legions falling:
Spring's three-month handiwork before the wind in flight,
A day-dream of pear-blossom on a moonlit night.
...

(*Hawkes' translation*)

The meaning of poetry is multi-dimensional to different readers. "明月", "梅花" and "一梦" put together will surely form different pictures in different readers' minds. If they are translated into English on the basis of hypotaxis, then those different pictures turn into a single one. The juxtaposition of these images enables readers employ the imagination infinitely. As a result, the two translators translated this line respectively into "Moonlight and plum-blossom nothing but a dream" and "A day-dream of pear-blossom on a moonlit night". The same verse produces two entirely different translated versions. "It is not because translators use different dictionaries, but because imagine differently." (刘雪芹, 2007 : 147. the translation is mine.)

7.2.2. Succinctness

Being the most condensed and concentrated form of literature, poetry conveys the most in the fewest number of words. Chinese is not burdened with tenses, genders or cases, subjects, predicates, or conjunctions are usually omitted in Chinese poetry; in addition, words can be inverted and part of speech can be changed, all of which are beneficial to the composition of poems. In classical Chinese poems, the language detaches itself from these restrictions, and the things or experiences are presented directly or naturally, without any texts inserted. So language in Chinese poetry is simple and rich in connotations. The following poem will well illustrate this:

Example 40:

ST:

南柯子

空挂纤纤缕,徒垂络络丝,也难绾系也难羁,一任东西南北各分离.

落去君休惜,飞来我自知. 莺愁蝶倦晚芳时,纵是明春再见隔年期!

(《红楼梦》第七十回)

In the first part, both "纤纤缕" and "络络丝" refer to the "willow's branches"; "空挂""徒垂" are similar expressions and so are "绾""羁". Due to the omission of the subject and lack of pronouns, the lines can be interpreted as the description of the willow's slenderness and drifting or the poet's vagrant life and gloomy mood. As to the pronouns "君" and "我" in the next sentence, different readers may have different interpretations. Who is "君"? and who is "我"?, which put the readers and the translators in an embarrassing situation. Perceived from different angles, the lines "落去君休惜,飞来我自知" may acquire different significance. Since "落去" and "飞来" can only refer to “柳絮”, some possibilities of significance are presented in the table below: (刘雪芹, 2007: 147)

Table 7.2 The possible signified in the poem

表达者（主语）	落去	君	休懔（主语）	飞来	我	自知
诗人 柳絮		读者	柳絮	诗人	自己知道	
柳絮 我		读者	我		柳絮	自然知道
	落去	柳絮	休懔			
柳树 柳絮		柳絮	柳絮	飞来	柳树	自然知道
		读者				

TT1:

In vain the willow trails long slender branches,
Hanging strands of silk are they;
They cannot curb the catkins
And north, south, east and west these drift away...
Do not mourn their falling;
Where they fly, only I have any idea;
Orioles grieve, butterflies flag as flowers fade,
But next spring, another year past, they will reappear.

(*Yang's translation*)

TT2:

Once in the air you start,
The creatures of the wind, the breezes' sport,
Not to be bound or held back by any art,

To north and south and east and west
You drift apart.
Your drifting fate not fear;
I understand the message that you bear.
Though orioles mourn and the flowers' end seems near,
Spring will return, but I must wait
Another year.

(*Hawkes' translation*)

The fuzziness in the original and the concreteness in the translated versions show different choices of persons and viewpoint. In the first part of Yang's translation, the separation of willow and catkins is perceived from the angle of a spectator (poet). In the second part, still the poet says "Don't mourn their falling; where they fly, only I have any idea" to the readers, while Hawkes regards willows as listeners, and catkins as listenees in the whole poem, which greatly differs from Yang's.

The multivalence of poetry which allows ample room for imagination has to be reduced to univalence in the translation process because several pictures produced by the juxtaposition of images have to be restricted to one picture; subjectless sentences in Chinese have to be given a subject, and sentences unburdened with tenses have to be fixed at a certain time. While the indeterminacy and simplicity determine various interpretations, it can be concluded that "if translation process is also an interpretative process, then different translations are different text interpretations. Provided they are rational, they are acceptable." (刘雪芹, 2007: 150. The translation is mine.) It's generally known that English is focused on subject and Chinese is concentrated on topics. Because Chinese is a parataxis-prominent language, omission of subjects provides more interpretive room for translators instead of making the readers bewildered, different techniques may be used in transferring the point of view from the SL to TL. As illustrated in the above example, different choices of subjects affect the translators' choice of viewpoint. As Wang Li said, "On rare occasions some incomplete sentences appear in prose, while in poetry they are frequent. Poetic language as the most condensed one has to manifest vast pictures in just dozens of words, so many structures of sentences are forced to be condensed. The so-called incomplete sentences refer to the sentences without predicates or with incomplete predicates, the most obvious ones are noun sentences, which means a noun phrase is a sentence." (王力, 2000: 140-141. The translation is mine.) As a result, much space left in each line by the poet awaits readers to fill it in and externalize it, which gives the translators the right to interpret and fill in their own understanding with the form of expression of the ST during the process of concretization, hence, different translated versions are produced on the basis of the same ST.

7.2.3 Implicitness

Poetry should be implicit rather than explicit. Implicitness makes every use of the implication and allusion to arouse the readers' imagination so as to experience and discover the profound and provoking taste from the works. Implied meaning is associated with the context, culture, tradition or it is something that the author deliberately hides behind words. Classical Chinese poetry is good at employing allusions and implication, etc., and focuses on implied meaning, which requires the poetry to fuel the readers' endless imagination with limited words and sentences. Chinese language with a specially flexible grammar enables the writing to keep flexible and free, with readers centered on "neither friendly nor aloof" and the writing like the things in real life that provides some room for us to act freely and get in and out form different angles.

The language of *Hongloumeng* is vivid, elegant and concise, and has widespread and profound cultural connotation, which demonstrates the author possesses a depth of knowledge of both Chinese language and culture. As the bridge between the SL and TL, firstly a translator should conduct a careful study of the original as a reader, inevitably he understands the original with a little of his own brand during this process. Then he represents the original as the author of the translation, and gives his own special style to his translation. Only with the translator's interpretation of the original as a reader, can the original get the fresh image and proper meaning, and can the work's indeterminacy and gaps be revealed and filled. Translation is the product of translator's interpretation of the original in his own way and expression in his own language. So difference in translated versions is inevitable.

7.3 Subjectivity—as an undeniable fact

"主观性" and "主体性" are both expressed by the word "subjectivity" in English. Subjectivity (主体性) is the most essential quality of the subject reflected in its reaction towards the object. To be more exact, it is the externalization of the subject's innate capacity in his objectified activities, the distinctive features that the subject possesses to change, influence and manipulate his object and makes the object serve itself. It includes the subject's motivation, creation, initiative spirit and other factors, among which the initiative is the most salient one. Many scholars have made subtle distinctions between "主观性" and "主体性", from their perspectives, they tend to associate "主观性" with man's spiritual conscious state, and associate "主体性" with human practice and activity to the objective world; in the meantime, it's generally considered that "主体性" covers a wider range than "主观性", that's to say, "主观性" is a part of "主体性". But in Chinese linguistic circles, scholars usually use "主观性" instead of distinguishing between these two concepts.

In this thesis subjectivity (主观性) will be used, which, in my opinion emphasizes subjective desire and autonomy (主观意愿性) and comprises language subjectivity and translator's subjectivity. Both the language and translator bear subjectivity, which is not always a subjective conjecture, but a thinking mode of translation and a manifestation of subjective initiative of translation subject. Language and translator's subjectivity run through the translation process and affect the translator's different translation approaches.

7.3.1 Language subjectivity

Language is indispensable to translation. In translation, the language acts as both content and form. The operation of language is the prerequisite of translation, so virtually translation is a special case during the generalized language process. In the West the linguistic translation theories that hold a leading post in contemporary translation theories argue that translation should belong to linguistic categories and language attributes determine translation attributes. Luo Su once said, "Language has the functions of expressing and communicating." (罗素, 2008: 70. The translation is mine.) It is not necessary that without language, there can be no thought, but the expression of thought has to depend on language. In addition, the choice and the use of language often influence the expressive effect. Thus, language attributes exert a fundamental, profound and overall influence on translation as inter-cultural communication.

Firstly, language meaning is subjective. Language subjectivity has been an important category in philosophy and linguistics since the philosophical "linguistic turn", to which high attention has been attached by cognitive linguistics, functional linguistics and pragmatics. The linguist Benveniste is believed to have clearly defined subjectivity(主观性) earlier from the perspective of language. He defines it as the following, "The subjectivity (主观性) is the capacity of the speaker to posit himself as "subject". It is defined not by the feeling which everyone experiences of being himself (this feeling, to the degree that it can be taken note of, is only a reflection) but as the psychic unity that transcends the totality of the actual experiences it assembles and that makes the permanence of the consciousness. Now we hold that the "subjectivity", whether it is placed in phenomenology or in psychology, as one may wish, is only the emergence in the being of a fundamental property of language. "Ego" is he who says "ego". That is where we see the foundation of "subjectivity", which is determined by the linguistic status of "person." (Benveniste, 1971: 224) This definition not only lies in expressing oneself, but also implies that man is the foundation of subject existence, and this foundation is realized by language. Namely, language is no longer the tool man manipulates. After that another linguist Lyons further states, "In making an utterance, the speaker simultaneously comments upon that utterance and expresses his attitude to what he is saying." (Lyons, 1977: 739) That's to say, the speaker is expressing his attitude, views and emotion to it when making an utterance, hence leaving his own imprint in the utterance. It means that on one hand, polysemy and fuzziness are ubiquitous in language; on the other hand, language symbol is characterized as arbitrariness, and meaning is different from person to person. The display of language subjectivity can be shown from the speaker's perspective, emotion and cognition, which deals with sentence patterns, deixis, tense, modality, mood and discourse markers etc, in a way, language subjectivity is embodied at different language levels.

Secondly, language meaning is relative. Language meaning is fixed in a certain context. Wittgenstein believes that language usage is a kind of language game, like playing chess and playing cards, which shares similarity rather than generality in all kinds of games including language games. Seen in this light, words and concepts often used haven't fixed and determinate meaning, they exist in "language games", which indicates that their meanings are to be decided according to concrete and special conditions and occasions. Everyone has his own understanding and has his own "Hamlet" in his eye, as is the same to "There are a thousand Hamlets in a thousand people's eyes." said by Shakespeare. Obviously, language understanding is associated with a linguistic knower, whose cultural background, emotion, knowledge and experience and other subjective elements form a part of context during the process of understanding, thus turns into realistic factors of understanding.

Lastly, language moves between the continuum of "telling through words" and "tacit understanding" when conveying meaning. Translation from one language to another language is essentially language communication among people, but not all is conveyed by language. Indeed, a part of knowledge is understood by "telling through words" and some by "tacit understanding". Knowledge by "tacit understanding" is interrelated with specific subject, and permeated with the subject's emotion, desire, needs and motive etc, instead of mere rationality, which can only be perceived by the subject's various psychological mechanism and individual unique experience. So inevitably it is burdened with individual subjectivity.

7.3.2 Translator's subjectivity

Translation would be impossible without the role of translator's subjectivity or his recognition and re-expression of the things that the original writer has understood. A good translation work is not only the fruit of the recognition and re-expression, but also felicitous display of the translator's subjectivity. To carry out research on the subjectivity of the translator, we must firstly have an understanding of the translating process. Translation is not merely the simple transference between the ST and TT. The formula should be like this: the author—the original text —the translator— the target text— the readers. In the whole process, firstly the translator is the reader of the ST who tries to construct a mental conception of the original text. He uses as an input to the translation process information, which would normally be the output and therefore the end of the reading process. So he should receive the maximum information from the ST. But no matter how hard he tries, he still can't exhaust the meanings of the text. And the understanding of the text varies among different translators owing to their different life experience, aesthetic attitudes, language competence, cultural awareness, etc. Secondly, he is to be a formulator or a writer in the target language. As Dryden described, he has to "dance on ropes with fettered legs." (Snell-Hornby, 2001: 11) In the translating process, he has to think about the reception of the translation. The differences between languages create more chances for their creativity. As the scholar Xu Jun says, "No matter in the understanding of the original text or in the expression in the target, the translator plays the primary role [...] the subjective factors of the translator including his personality, temperament, talents, cultural awareness, background knowledge, competence in language use, even his social position and ethnic choice will exert direct and significant influence in translation." (quoted in 邓丽君, 2005: 8)

Since translator's subjectivity objectively exists, different translation approaches and strategies may be used by different translators in the process of translation, which results in different versions even to the same original. So is the case in the translation of *Hongloumeng*.

It goes without saying that human beings differ from each other in endless ways due to different heredity, nature, environment or nurture. As is discussed before, the translator's subjectivity is manifested during the whole translation process. Through large amount of facts that one single ST has various versions in the same target language, it is not difficult to find that different translators show different inclinations and make different decisions and choices during translation. According to Michael, W. Eysenck, one of the United Kingdom's most prominent psychologists, heredity and environment both play an important part in producing individual differences in behavior. (Eysenck, 2002: 34) In his book *Simply Psychology*, Eysenck suggested eight factors determining human beviour:

• the specific stimuli presented to us;

• the specific endowment: what we have inherited from our parents;

• our physiological system;

• our cognitive system (our perceptions, thoughts and memories);

• the social environment;

• the cultural environment;

• our previous life experience;

• our personal characteristics (including intelligence, personality and mental health). (Eysenck, 2002: 3)

It is quite clear that it is impossible to find any two people who possess the same eight factors summarized above. A translator is a component of human society, and translation is an activity. According to the concepts put forward by Eysenck, the fact that not any two translators may share the same nature or nurture at the same time shows the reason why different translators render different versions to the same ST. The poetry translation of *Hongloumeng* is one of the cases.

It was not until the 1970s that *Hongloumeng* was introduced completely to the West by Yang Xianyi and his wife Gladys Yang as well as David Hawkes and his son-in-law John Minford.

David Hawkes, a British Sinologist studying Chinese in Oxford University, after graduation with Chinese as the second bachelor degree in 1948, then continued to major in classical Chinese literature in Beijing University for 3 years. With great achievements in Chinese language and culture as a native English speaker, he was fascinated by the great work *Hongloumeng*. Coming back to Britain, he resigned from Oxford University and exerted himself whole-heartedly on the translation of *Hongloumeng*. He translated the first 80 chapters and his son-in-law, John Minford, an Australian Sinologist, translated the rest 40 chapters.

Nearly at the same time when Hawkes was devoting himself fully to the translation of *Hongloumeng*, Yang Xianyi and his wife Gladys Yang in China were making the same endeavor, too. Yang Xianyi, a Chinese translator, went to Britain to study ancient Greek and Roman literature, French literature and English literature in Oxford University. He and his wife Gladys Yang enjoy great fame in the Chinese academia especially in the field of translation.

Though both Yang and Hawkes are knowledgeable and have a good command of Chinese, their translation style is extremely different. The reasons are attributed to the difference in translator's subjectivity, the factors are that Yang was born in China; Hawkes was born in an English-speaking country. Yang's native language is Chinese; Hawkes' is English. They two immersed in diversely different religious backgrounds, etc.

Example 41:

ST:

……

似这般,生关死劫谁能躲?

闻说道,西方宝树唤婆娑,上结着长生果。

（《红楼梦》第五回）

TT1:

Who can escape the gate of birth, the fate of death?
Yet the west, they say, grows the sal tree
Which bears the fruit of immortality.

(*Yang's translation*)

TT2:

The doors of life and death all must go through.
Yet this I know is true:
In Paradise there grows a precious tree
Which bears the fruit of immortality.

(*Hawkes'translation*)

In this poem, "西方宝树", "婆娑" and "长生果" are all fundamental concepts of Buddhism. "西方宝树" and "婆娑" is the legendary tree where Buddha Sakyamuni obtained his Buddhahood, serving in Chinese culture as a symbol of devotion to Buddhism. "长生果" as the fruit of the legendary tree bestows people immortality. These three concepts imply that Xichun will finally turn into a nun. The dominant religious consciousness of individual translator inevitably demonstrates itself obviously in this case. Yang who comes from the same cultural and religious background of the author of Cao Xueqin empathizes to the author and the ST and literally renders these concepts. On the other hand, Hawkes replaces the Buddhist legendary world with the image "paradise" that is the dwelling place the Lord creates for the ancestors Adam and Eve in the western religion. Paradise, as an image with intensive western religious sense in Hawkes' mind, reoccurs in his translation as the following:

Example 42:

ST:

一个是阆苑仙葩，一个是美玉无瑕。

（《红楼梦》第五回）

TT1:

One is an immortal flower of fairylang,
The other fair flawless jade.

(*Yang's translation*)

TT2:

One was a flower from paradise,
One a pure jade without spot or stain.

(*Hawkes' translation*)

Once again, we see in Hawkes' translation the image "paradise" replacing fairyland conveying strong Chinese legendary sense as an intentionally easier way for the western readers to understand by empathizing to the readers. These differences in translation caused by individual religious consciousness testify the manipulative power of the translator's subjectivity.

Conclusion

This dissertation highlights the significance of applying the approach of empathy to the translation of classical Chinese poetry represented by the poetry in *Hongloumeng* and makes a comparative study of the two versions of translation of poems in *Hongloumeng* in the light of the approach of empathy. It begins with a general survey of the empathetic approach, introducing the historical development and the definition of empathy and making a comparison between Chinese and Western empathy. In addition, the author's view of the possibility of translation is stated; the difficulties of poetry translation caused by linguistic, grammar and cultural differences are mentioned; and then the theoretical and practical foundations of the application of the approach of empathy in poetry translation are narrated. A comparison of aesthetic empathy in poetry translation in *Hongloumeng* is made along with a comparison of cultural empathy and pragmatic empathy. In the comparative study, it is shown that Yang mainly empathizes towards the ST and the author, and the language of his translation faithfully conveys the original's rich and profound connotations so that English readers may find it hard to adapt to such form, technique or mood. On the contrary, Hawkes mainly empathizes towards the TT and the readers, and some contents are even rewritten. Some poems, in the form of English ballads, with beautiful sound, form and mood, are fluent and easy for westerners to read and understand.

Through the systematic comparison, an exploration is made into the factors that influence the two translator's approaches in poetry translation in *Hongloumeng*. The focus of the dissertation is not the comparison or the evaluation of which translated version is better. Rather, it aims to try to find out why the two translators have adopted different approaches. And the cognition of these factors may benefit us in our understanding of the differences in the two English versions.

From the above explanations, we may well assume that the approaches adopted by Yang and Hawkes in translating *Hongloumeng* are closely related to the following factors:

Firstly, some translation theories provide theoretic explanations of different empathetic approaches, such as skopos theory, hermeneutics and deconstruction view. Skopos theory makes it possible for translators to translate in different approaches in order to gain their different translating purpose; hermeneutics justifies the display of translators' differences in the understanding and expressing stages in translating activity. When translators approach the same original, they may derive various interpreted meanings from the ST owing to their own fore-understanding and prejudice, which will lead to the plurality of interpretations and diversity of translations; and deconstruction view declares the translators are subjects of translation, illustrates the necessity of the translators' subjective initiative, and promotes the status of the translators in translating in a theoretical sense. The above-mentioned three theories do justify theoretically the two different empathetic approaches of Yang's and Hawkes'.

Secondly, features of Chinese poetic language allow for expansion. Chinese poetry has its own characteristics, such as vividness, succinctness and implicitness, which allow for expansion on the basis of translators' understanding.

Thirdly, subjectivity(主观性) is not only inevitable but even indispensable. Language subjectivity and translators' subjectivity (主观性) penetrate the translation process and affect the translators' different translation approaches.

These are likely to explain why their translations differ. All in all, as far as translation approaches are concerned, we can't say which one is better, or which one is worse. The adoption should be determined according to different factors on the purpose of producing a good translation. This dissertation may serve as a reference for the re-evaluation of the phenomenon of literary re-translation. We should be aware that the comparison and competition among various versions can enhance our appreciation of the original flavor from varying angles. The author sincerely hopes that studies conducted in this dissertation can also be a good support for relevant studies on translation criticism and amendments of translation criteria.

Since this dissertation is a tentative analysis of the approach of empathy in poetry translation in *Hongloumeng*, due to the author's limitation of knowledge and perspectives, what has been done in this dissertation is far from perfect. Some limitations and problems are inevitable. The dissertation awaits further improvement.

Firstly, in this dissertation, the author can only choose a limited number of poems as examples. And the selection and comparison of these examples is inevitable with some personal biases to some extent. The analysis is somewhat subjective though the author tries to be objective.

Secondly, this study only focuses on the aesthetic, cultural and pragmatic analysis of empathy. In fact, empathy can also be studied from other angles, such as sociolinguistics and intercultural communication, to make the analysis more comprehensive and penetrative.

Lastly, the explanations that account for the two different empathetic approaches are not exhausted, and it is inevitable that divergence between the two versions is not just caused by these factors that the author has mentioned.

With the discussion of both findings and limitations of this dissertation, it is hoped that this study will help people use empathy in some other relevant studies. The author hopes that the follow-up researchers will deepen the understanding of empathy and broaden its application to more linguistic genres.

Bibliography

Abrams, M. H. *The Norton Anthology of English Literature* [M] (7th Edition, Vol. 2). New York: W. W. Norton & Company, 1999.

Baker, M. *Routledge Encyclopedia of Translation Studies* [M]. London and New York: Routledge, 1998.

Barnstone, W. *The Poetics of Translation* [M]. New Haven and London: Yale University Press, 1993.

Basch, M. F. Empathic Understanding: A Review of the Concept and Some Theoretical Considerations [J]. *Journal of the American Psychoanalytic Association*: 1983, 31.

Bassnett, S. & Lefevere, A. *Constructing Cultures: Essays on Literary Translation* [M]. Shanghai: Shanghai Foreign Language Education Press, 2004.

Bassnett, S. *Translation Studies* (3rd Edition) [M]. London and New York: Routledge, Taylor & Francis Group, 2005.

Bennett, M. J. *Handbook of Intercultural Training* (3rd Edition) [M]. Beijing: Peking University Press, 2004.

Bennett, M. J. *Basic Concepts of Intercultural Communication: Selected Readings* [M]. Yarmouth, Maine: Intercultural Press, Inc, 1998.

Benveniste, E. *Problems in General Linguistics* [M]. Coral Gables, Florid: University of Miami press, 1971.

Bonnefoy, Y. *Translating Poetry* [M]. Chicago and London: University of Chicago Press, 1989.

Brian, O. *Longman Dictionary of Contemporary English* [M]. Essex: Longman Group UK Limited, 1995.

Brown, H. D. *Principles of Language Learning and Teaching* [M]. New Jersey: Prentice-Hall, Inc, 1987.

Chan Sin-wai and Pollard, D. E. *An Encyclopaedia of Translation* [M]. Hong Kong: The Chinese University Press, 1995.

Cao, X. Q. *The Story of the Stone* [M] (tr. by Hawkes, D.). London: Penguin Books Ltd., 1973.

Catford, J. C. *A Linguistic Theory of Translation* [M]. London: Oxford University Press, 1965.

Cuddon, J. A. *A Dictionary of Literary Terms* [M] (Revised Edition). London: Andre Deutch Ltd., 1979.

Davis, M. H. *Empathy: A Social Psychological Approach* [M]. Boulder, Colo: Westview Press, 1996.

Duan, C. & Hill, C. E. The Current State of Empathy Research [J]. *Journal of Counseling Psychology*, 1996, 43 (3): 261-274.

Eisenberg, N. & Strayer, J. *Empathy and its Development* [M]. New York: Cambridge University Press, 1987.

Eysenck, M. W. *Simply Psychology* (2nd Edition) [M]. East Sussex: Psychology Press Ltd., 2002.

Fussell, P. *Poetic Meters and Poetic Form* [M]. New York: Random House, 1965.

Gadamer, H. G. *Truth and Method* [M]. (tr. by Barden, G. & Cumming, J.). Beijing: China Social Sciences Publishing House, 1975.

Gadamer, H. G. *Philosophical Hermeneutics* [M]. Berkeley: University of California Press, 1976.

Goldstein, A. P. & Michaels, G. Y. *Empathy: Development, Training, and Consequences* [M]. Hillsdale, New Jersey: Lawrence Erlbaum Associates, 1985.

Gill, R. *Mastering English Literature* [M]. Basingstoke, Hampshire: Macmillan Education Ltd., 1985.

Hanvey, R. G. *An Attainable Global Perspective* [M]. New York: Center for Global Perspectives, 1979.

Hatim, B. & Munday, J. *Translation: An Advanced Resource Book* [M]. London and New York: Routledge, 2004.

Hatim, B. &. Mason, I. *Discourse and the Translator* [M]. Shanghai: Shanghai Foreign Language Education Press, 2001.

Hawkes, D. *The Story of the Stone* [M]. London: Penguin Books Ltd., 1973 , 1977 , 1980.

Heidegger, M. *Being and Time* [M]. (tr. by Macquarrie, J. & Robinson, E.). Beijing: China Social Science Publishing House, 1999.

Hogan, R. T. Development of an Empathy Scale [J]. *Journal of Consulting Psychology*, 1969, vol. 33, 307-316.

Hornby, A. S. *Oxford Advanced Learner's English Chinese Dictionary* [M]. Beijing: The Commercial Press, 2002.

Kennedy, X. J. *An Introduction to Poetry* [M]. Boston: Little Brown and Company Ltd., 1986.

Kirszner, L. G. & Mandell, S. R. *Literature: Reading, Reacting, Writing* [M]. U.S.A.: Harcout Brace College Publishers, 1997.

Laurence, P. *Sound and Sense: An Introduction to Poetry* [M]. New York: Harcount, Brace and World, Inc, 1969.

Lee, V. *The Beautiful: An Introduction to Psychological Aesthetics* [M]. Cambridge: Cambridge University Press, 1913.

Lefevere, A. *Translation, Rewriting, and the Manipulation of Literary Fame* [M]. London and New York: Routledge, 1992.

Lyons, J. *Semantics* (Vol. 2) [M]. Cambridge: Cambridge University Press, 1977.

Mead, G. H. *Mind, Self and Society* [M]. Chicago: University of Chicago Press, 1934.

Munday, J. *Introducing Translation Studies: Theory and Application* [M]. London: Routledge, 2001.

Meyer, M. *Poetry: An Introduction* [M]. New York: Bedford Books of ST. Martin's Press, 1967.

Newmark, P. *A Textbook of Translation* [M]. Shanghai: Shanghai Foreign Language Education Press, 2001.

Nida, E. A. *Toward a Science of Translating: with Special Reference to Principles and Procedures Involved in Bible*

Translating [M]. Leiden: E. J. Bill, 1964.

Nida, E. A. Approaches to Translating in the Western World [J]. *Foreign Language Teaching and Research*, 1984 (2): 9-15.

Nida, E. A. *Language and Culture: Contexts in Translating* [M]. Shanghai: Shanghai Foreign Language Education Press, 2001a.

Nida, E. A. *Language, Culture, and Translating* [M]. Shanghai: Shanghai Foreign Language Education Press, 2001b.

Nida, E. A. & Taber, C. R. *The Theory and Practice of Translation* [M]. Leiden: E. J. Brill, 1982.

Nida, E. A. & Reyburn, W. D. *Meaning across Cultures* [M]. Maryknoll, N.Y : Obris, 1981.

Nord, C. *Translating as a Purposeful Activity: Functionalist Approaches Explained* [M]. Shanghai: Shanghai Foreign Language Education Press, 2001.

Ogden, C. K. & Richards, I. A. *The Meaning of Meaning* [M]. New York: Harcourt, 1923.

Parini, J. *An Invitation to Poetry* [M]. Englewood: Prentice-Hall, 1987.

Partridge, A. C. & Donne, J. *Language and Style* [M]. Great Britain: W & J Mackay Limited, Chathan, 1978.

Perrine, L. *Sound and Sense: An Introduction to Poetry* (3rd Edition) [M]. New York: Harcourt, Brace & World, Inc, 1969.

Poupard, D. *Literature Criticism from 1400 to 1800* (Vol. 1) [M]. New Jersey: Gale Research Company, 1984.

Rader, M. Introductory Note. *A Modern Book of Esthetics: An Anthology* (3rd Edition) [M]. London: Holt, Rinehart and Winston Inc, 1960.

Raffel, B. *How to Read a Poem* [M]. New York: Penguin, 1984.

Raffel, B. *The Art of Translating Poetry* [M]. University Park and London: The Pennsylvania State University Press, 1988.

Reiss, K. & Vermeer, H. J. *Grundlegung Einer Allgemeinen Translations Theorie* [M]. Tubingen: Niemeyer, 1984.

Reiss, K. *Translation Criticism — The Potentials and Limitations* [M]. (tr. By Rhodes, E. F.). Shanghai: Shanghai Foreign Language Education Press, 2004.

Robins, R. H. *A Short History of Linguistics* [M]. London and New York: Longman, 1967.

Shakespeare, W. *The Tempest* [M]. London: Oxford University Press, 1914.

Schulte, R. & Biguenet, J. *Theories of Translation: An Anthology of Essays from Dryden to Derrida* [M]. Chicago: The University of Chicago Press, 1992.

Snell-Hornby, M. *Translation Studies: An Integrated Approach* [M]. Shanghai: Shanghai Foreign Language Education Press, 2001.

Stewart, J. *Interpretive Listening: An Alternative to Empathy* [M]. Communication Education, 1983, Vol. 32, 379-391.

Tylor, E. B. *Primitive Culture* [M]. London: John Murray, Albemarle Street, W. 1871.

Venuti, L. *The Translator's Invisibility: A History of Translation (Translation Studies)* [M]. London and New York: Routledge, 1995.

Vermeer, H. J. "What Does It Mean to Translate?" [J]. *Indian Journal of Applied Linguistics*. 1987, 13 (2): 25-33.

Vermeer, H. J. *Skopos and Translationsaufag-Aufsatze* [M]. Heidelberg: Universitat, 1989a.

Waard, J. & Nida, E. A. *From One Language to Another* [M]. Scotland: Thomas Nelson Inc, 1985.

Waley, A. *A Hundred and Seventy Chinese Poems* [M]. London: Constable and Co., 1917.

Whorf, B. L. *Language, Thought, and Reality* [M]. Selected Writings, edited by J. B. Carroll. Cambridge, Mass.: MIT Press, 1958.

Wilss, W. *The Science of Translation: Problems and Methods* [M]. Shanghai: Shanghai Foreign Language Education Press, 2001.

Wispé, L. *The Psychology of Sympathy* [M]. New York: Plenum Press, 1991.

Xu Yuanchong. *An Anthology of Classical Chinese Poetry* [M]. Beijing: New World Press, 1994.

Xu Yuanchong. *On Chinese Verse in English Rhyme* [M]. Beijing: Peking University Press, 1992.

Yang, X. Y. & Yang, G. *Poetry and Prose of the Tang and Song* [M]. Beijing: Chinese Literature Press, 1983.

Zhang, B. J. *A Critical Approach to Verse Translation from Chinese to English* [M]. Jinan: Foreign Languages School Shandong University, 1995.

Zhang, T. Z. & Wei, B. S. *100 Tang Poems* [M]. Beijing: China Translation and Publishing Corporation, 1990.

爱德华·萨丕尔.语言论：言语研究导论[M].陆卓元，译.北京：商务印书馆，1985.

伯特兰·罗素.我的哲学的发展[M].温锡增，译.北京：商务印书馆，2008.

蔡义江.红楼梦诗词[M].长春:吉林文史出版社，2005.

曹建辉.模糊语言学视阈下的《红楼梦》诗词翻译研究[D].中南大学，2009.

曹雪芹，高鹗.红楼梦[M].长沙：岳麓书社，1997.

常谢枫.中国古典诗翻译中格律的传达[J].《外语与翻译》，1995(2)：6—10.

陈文新，郭皓政.红楼梦诗词曲鉴赏[M].武汉：长江文艺出版社，2010.

陈佳楠.《红楼梦》文学与文化解读[M].杭州：杭州出版社，2017.

陈威.《红楼梦》中诗歌的两个英译本比较研究——以“三美”论为原则分析探析[D].衡阳：南华大学，2008.

陈彦. 浅析《红楼梦》诗词翻译中译者的主体意识 [J].长江大学学报(社会科学版)，2007(2)：100-101.

戴继国. 英国诗歌教程[M]. 北京：对外经济贸易大学出版社，2005.

邓丽君. 乔治·斯坦纳翻译四步骤理论光照下的译者主体性——评大卫·霍克斯和杨宪益、戴乃迭《红楼梦十二支曲》的翻译[D]. 武汉:武汉大学,2005.

邓炎昌,刘润清. 语言与文化[M]. 北京:外语教学与研究出版社,1989.

董学文,张永刚. 文学原理[M]. 北京:北京大学出版社,2001.

冯庆华. 红译艺坛:红楼梦翻译艺术研究[M]. 上海:上海外语教育出版社,2006.

郭锐,葛复庆. 红楼梦诗词赏析[M]. 武汉:崇文书局,2007.

辜正坤. 中西诗比较鉴赏与翻译理论[M]. 北京:清华大学出版社,2003.

顾正阳. 古诗词曲英译论稿[M]. 上海:百家出版社,2003.

韩雨苇. 东坡词英译赏识——审美移情视角[D]. 上海:上海外国语大学,2010.

何素芳. 论后殖民视阈下的《红楼梦》诗歌翻译策略[D]. 长沙:中南大学,2007.

何自然. 言语交际中的语用移情[J]. 外语教学与研究,1991(4):11—15.

贺新辉. 红楼梦诗词鉴赏辞典[M]. 北京:紫禁城出版社,1990.

黄国文. 翻译研究的语言学探索——古诗词英译本的语言学分析[M]. 上海:上海外语教育出版社,2007.

黄河清.从跨文化角度看中国古典诗歌意象的翻译[D].上海:上海外国语大学,2008.

李端严,杨宪益.戴乃迭英译本《红楼梦》技巧赏析[J].《外语教学》,1988(3):51-60.

李晓红.文学翻译中的文化移情[J].《南通大学学报》(社会科学版),2006(2):74-78.

李晓红.诗歌翻译中的审美移情与艺术生成[D].杭州:浙江大学,2007.

林同华.美学心理学[M].杭州:浙江人民出版社,1987.

刘曼.《红楼梦》诗词中文化现象的翻译策略研究[D].武汉:华中科技大学,2006.

刘宓庆.翻译美学导论[M].北京:中国对外翻译出版公司,2005.

刘宓庆.翻译与语言哲学[M].北京:中国对外翻译出版公司,2007.

刘婧.社会符号学视域下《红楼梦》文化内容的英译——以杨译本和霍译本为例[M].北京:中央编译出版社,2014.

刘心爽.《浪花的起源》中的语用移情研究[D].长春:吉林大学,2009.

刘雪芹.句法不确定性与诗词翻译——以红楼梦柳絮词为例[J].广西民族大学学报(哲学社会科学版),2007(4):146-150.

刘玉梅.杨宪益夫妇英译红楼梦诗词曲赋研究[D].成都:四川大学,2004.

刘重德.文学翻译十讲[M].北京:中国对外翻译出版公

司,2003.

罗静.从语义翻译和交际翻译比较分析《红楼梦》中的诗词翻译[D].呼和浩特:内蒙古大学,2010.

罗素.《人类的知识——其范围与限度》[M].张金言,译.北京:商务出版社,2008.

罗显克.中西移情论之比较[J].南宁师范高等专科学校学报,1999(1):34-39.

米云辉.从语际翻译中看汉语古典诗歌翻译的抗译性及策略性叛逆[D].武汉:武汉理工大学,2004.

马娜.《红楼梦》诗词英译文的原功能分析[D].大连:辽宁师范大学,2005.

潘卫民,钱妮娜.文学翻译中译者的移情作用刍议[J].外语与外语教学2006(2):51-54.

秦希仁.林黛玉诗词两译本的比较研究[D].长沙:中南大学,2007.

任生名.杨宪益的文学翻译思想散记[J].中国翻译,1993(4):33-34.

孙文侠.《红楼梦》诗词翻译中的风格传递[D].西安:西安电子科技大学,2004.

童庆炳.现代心理美学[M].北京:中国社会科学出版社,1993.

王洪超.诗歌翻译中形式的再现[D].济南:山东大学,1999.

王国维.人间词话[M].上海:上海古籍出版社,2005.

王力.诗词格律[M].北京:中华书局,2000.

王军.《红楼梦》之律诗翻译比较[D]. 成都：四川师范大学，2002.

王维. 从互文性理论视角解读中国古典诗歌中的文化翻译[D]. 南京：南京师范大学，2008.

王以铸. 论诗之不可译——兼论译诗问题[A]. 翻译论集，北京：商务印书馆，1984：873-888.

王佐良. 翻译：思考与试笔[M]. 北京：外语教学与研究出版社，1990.

翁显良. 诗词翻译的艺术[M]. 北京：中国对外翻译出版公司，1987.

奚永吉. 文学翻译比较美学[M]. 武汉：湖北教育出版社，2001.

谢天振. 作者本意和本文本意——解释学理论与翻译研究[J]. 外国语，2000(3)：53-60.

许钧. 文学翻译的理论与实践：翻译对话录[M]. 南京：译林出版社，2001.

许渊冲. 翻译的艺术[M]. 北京：中国对外翻译出版公司，1984.

许渊冲. 文学与翻译[M]. 北京：北京大学出版社，2003.

许渊冲. 唐宋词一百首[M]. 北京：中国对外翻译出版社，2007.

许渊冲. 唐诗三百首（中英文对照）[M]. 北京：中国对外翻译出版公司，2009.

徐丹. 文化融合中的语言翻译问题[J]. 中国翻译，1998(3)：2-5.

徐家昌.《红楼梦》诗词的特点[J]. 湖北大学学报(哲学社会科学版),1996(4):62-64.

袁锦翔. 王佐良翻译观之我见——《翻译:思考与试笔》读后感[J]. 外国语,1992(2):25-29,64,80.

袁锦翔.《名家翻译研究与赏析》[M]. 武汉:湖北教育出版社,1990.

杨宪益,戴乃迭.《红楼梦》(汉英对照)[M]. 北京:外文出版社, 1993.

张卫萍、赵春燕. 从语用移情看"红诗"的英译[J]. 顺德职业技术学院学报,2009(3):53-56.

张艳. 从目的论看《红楼梦》中的诗词翻译[D]. 合肥:安徽大学,2007.

张毅. 从许渊冲"三美"原则角度论李白诗歌英译的美感再现[D]. 哈尔滨:哈尔滨工程大学,2007.

周钰良. 周钰良文集[M]. 北京:外语教学与研究出版社, 1994.

朱慧芬. 从接受美学的角度对《红楼梦》诗歌英译的对比分析[D]. 杭州:浙江大学,2007.

朱光潜.《诗论》[M]. 合肥:安徽教育出版社, 1997.

朱徽. 中英比较诗艺[M]. 成都:四川大学出版社, 1996.

朱晓茜.《红楼梦》诗词曲赋两种英译文的对比和赏析[J]. 红楼梦学刊,1997(3):303-318.

卓正英. 汉诗英译中的移情[J]. 外语与外语教学,2001(1):53-55.

卓正英. 汉诗英译的总体审度与诗化[J]. 外语与外语教学,1997(4):44-46.